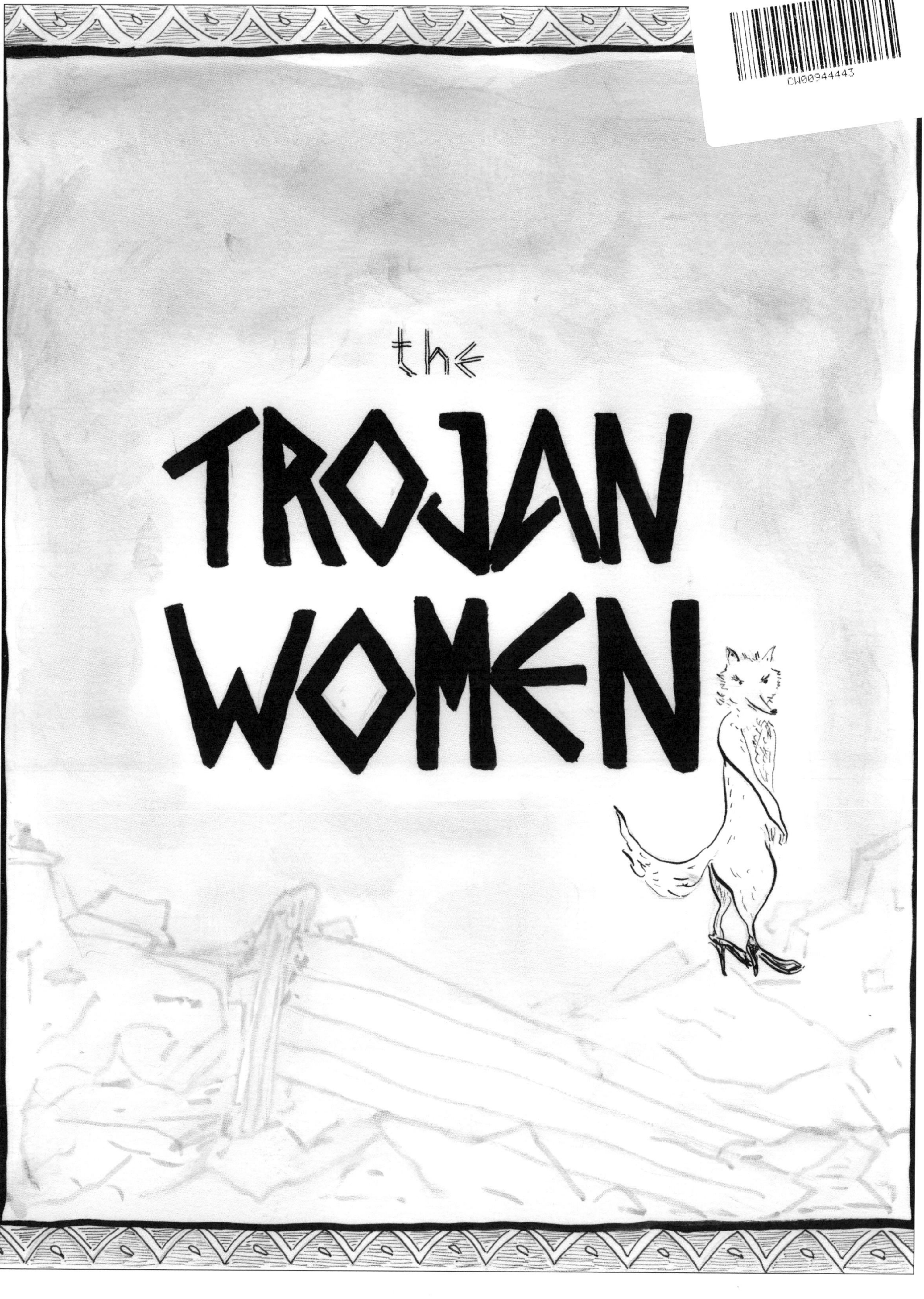
the
TROJAN
WOMEN

EURIPIDES

the TROJAN WOMEN

A COMIC

by ROSANNA BRUNO
text by ANNE CARSON

BLOODAXE BOOKS

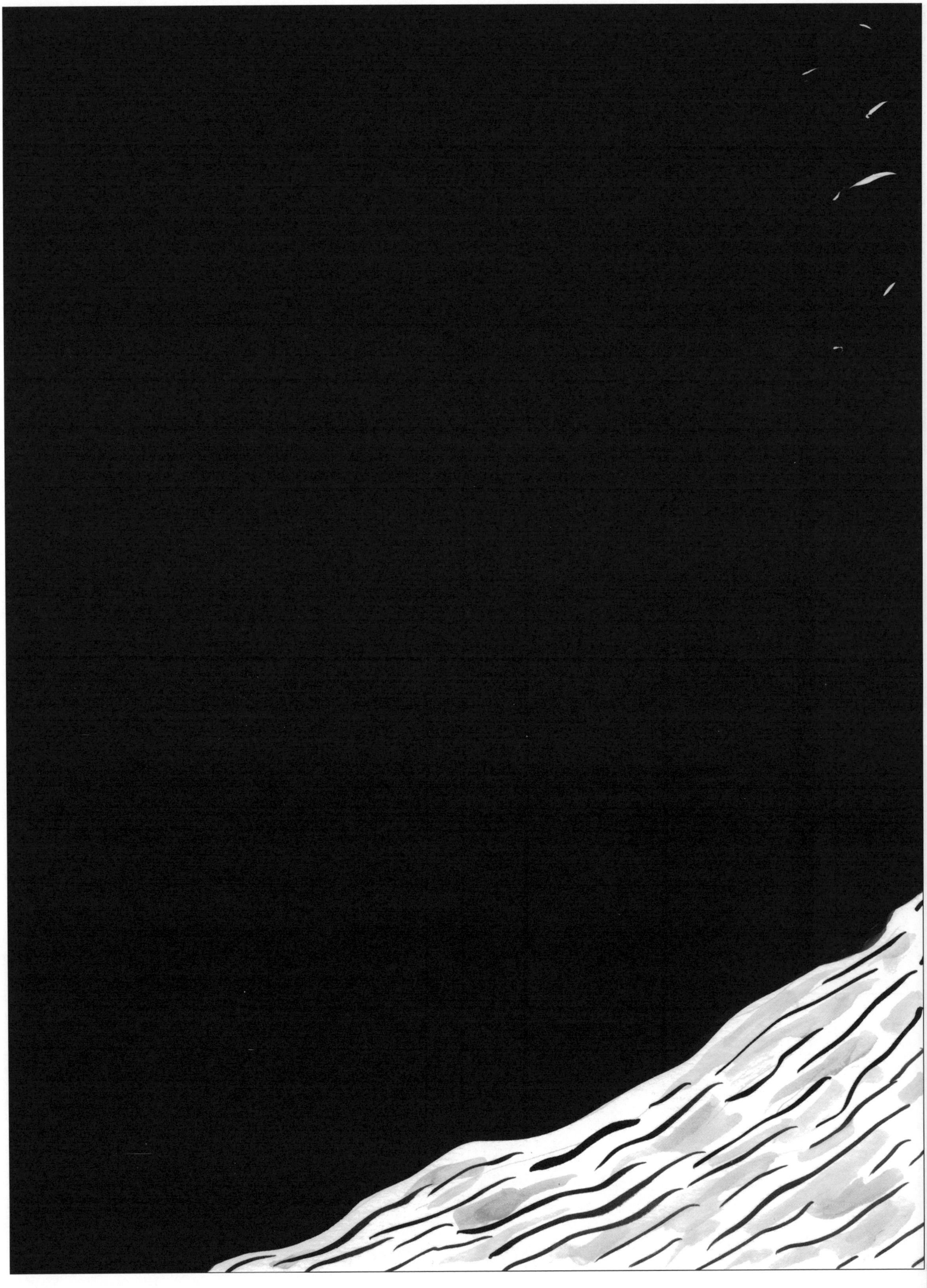

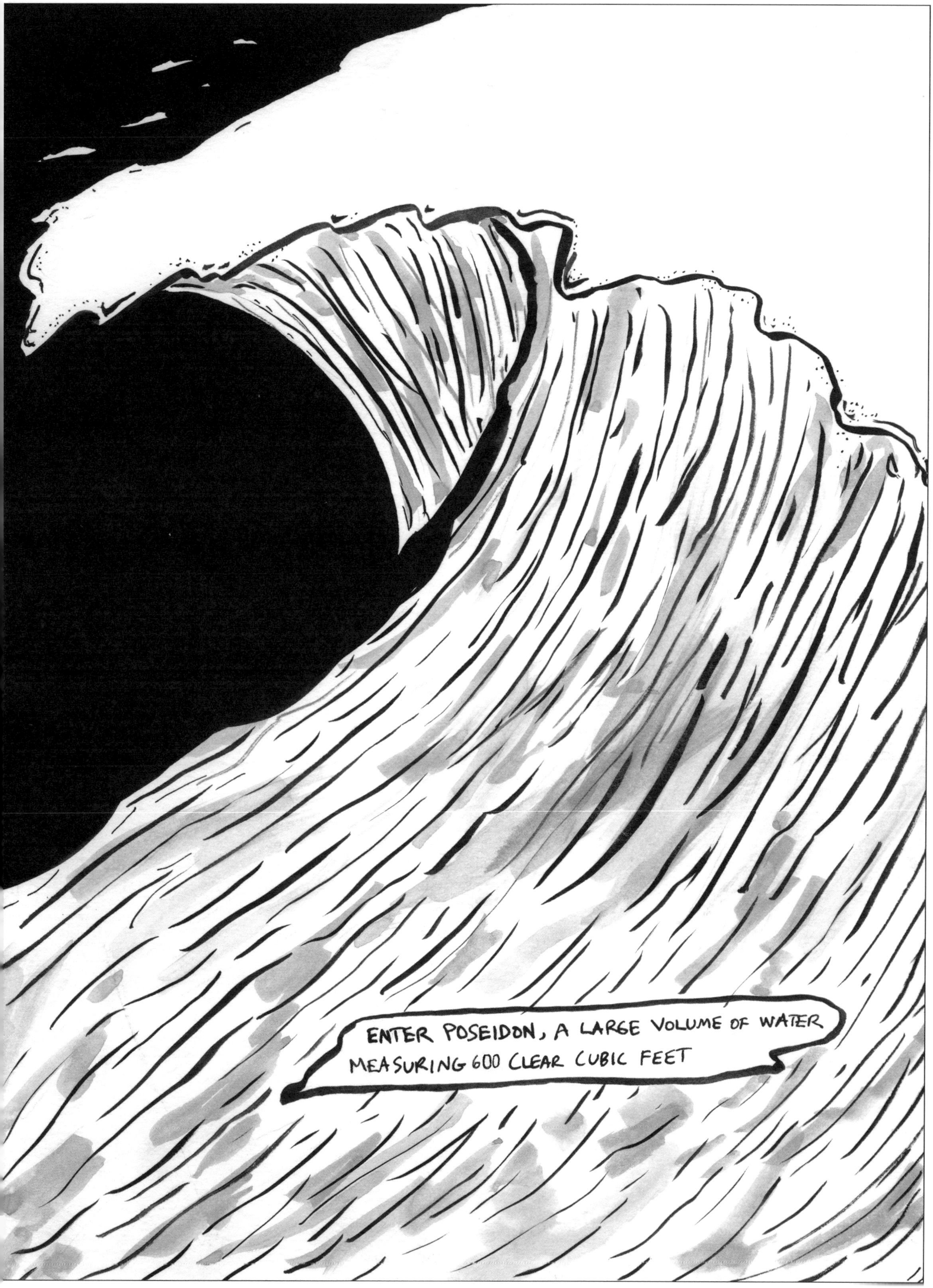
ENTER POSEIDON, A LARGE VOLUME OF WATER
MEASURING 600 CLEAR CUBIC FEET

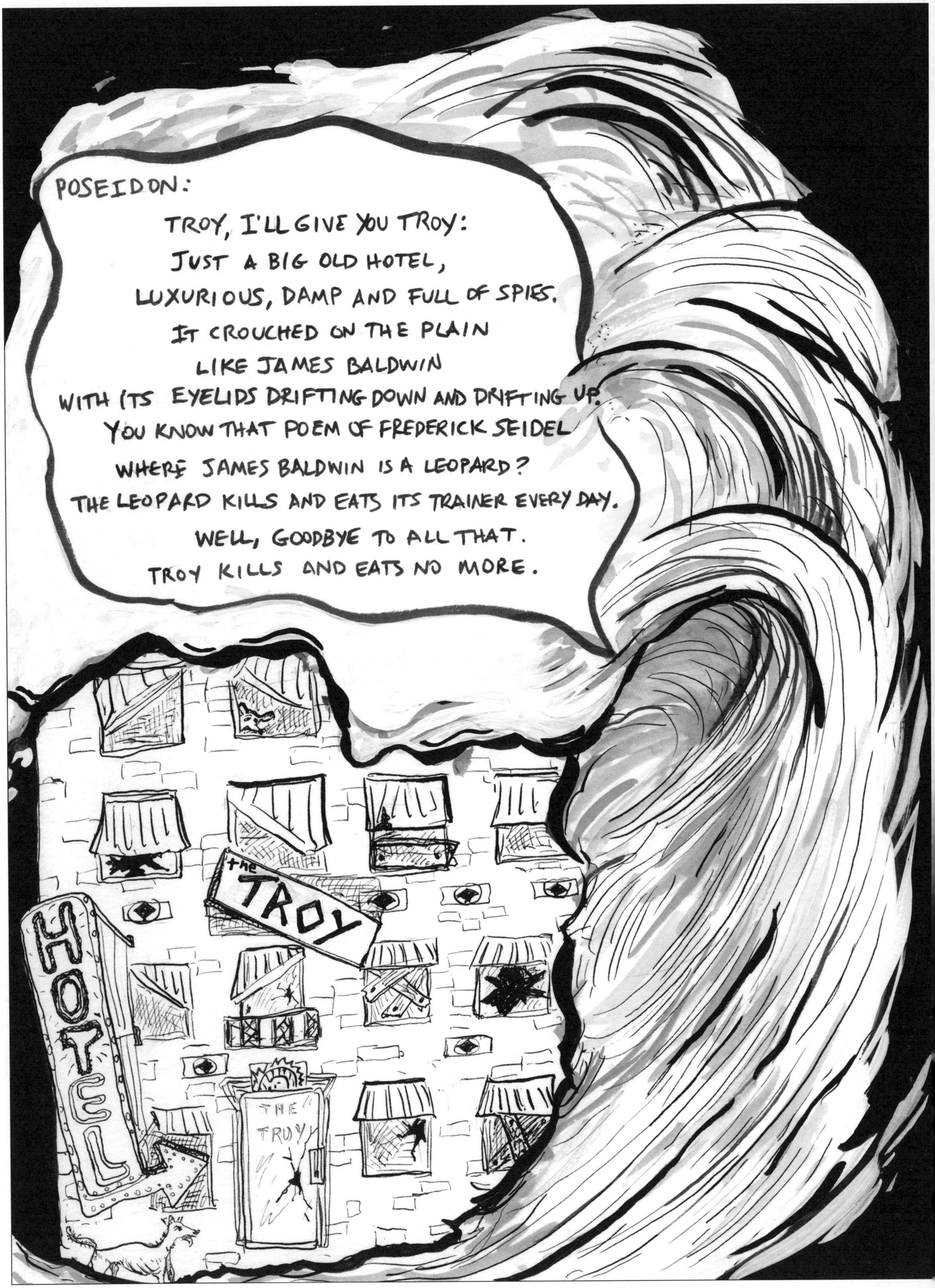
POSEIDON:
TROY, I'LL GIVE YOU TROY:
JUST A BIG OLD HOTEL,
LUXURIOUS, DAMP AND FULL OF SPIES.
IT CROUCHED ON THE PLAIN
LIKE JAMES BALDWIN
WITH ITS EYELIDS DRIFTING DOWN AND DRIFTING UP.
YOU KNOW THAT POEM OF FREDERICK SEIDEL
WHERE JAMES BALDWIN IS A LEOPARD?
THE LEOPARD KILLS AND EATS ITS TRAINER EVERY DAY.
WELL, GOODBYE TO ALL THAT.
TROY KILLS AND EATS NO MORE.
the TROY
HOTEL
THE TROY

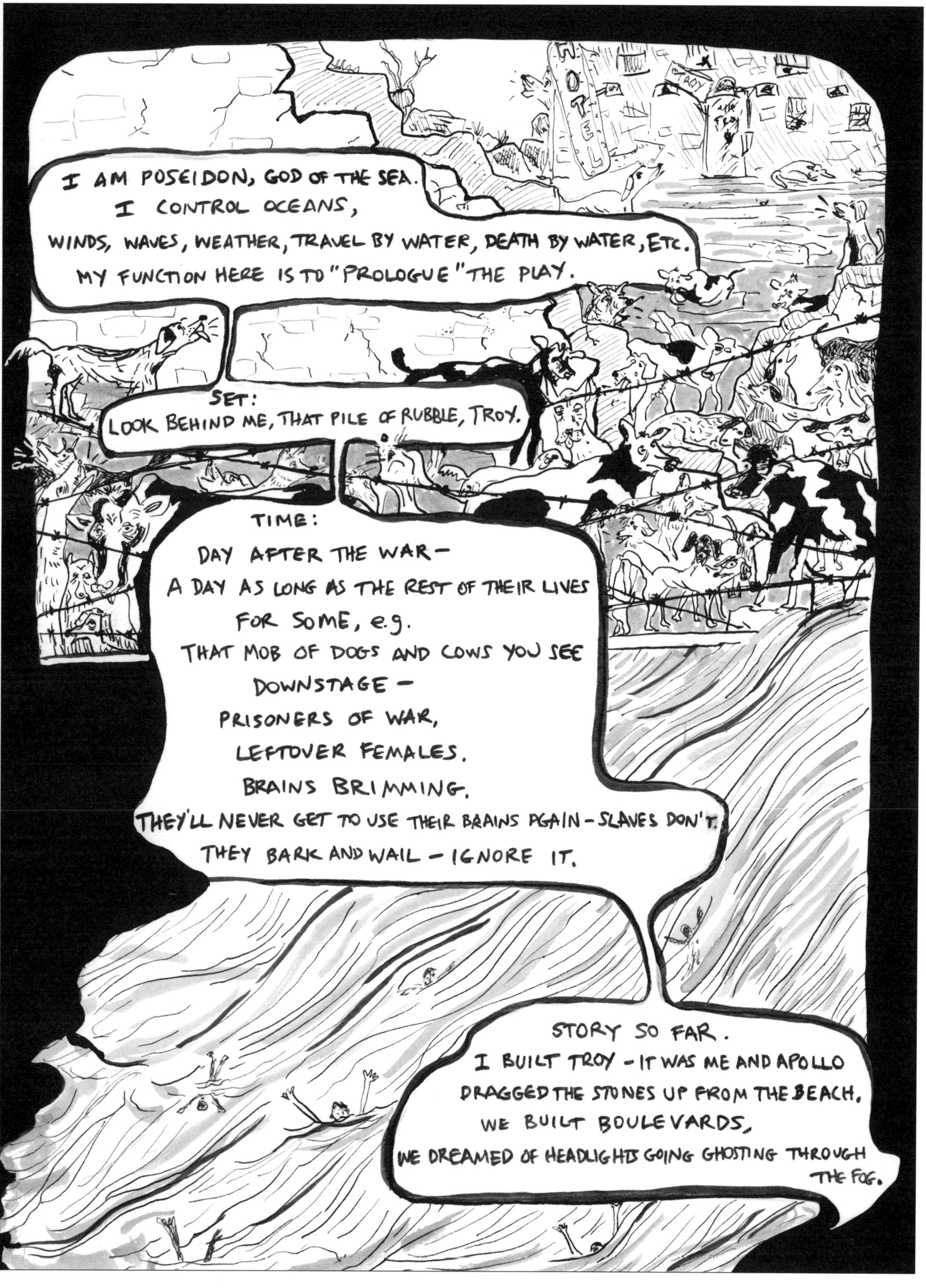
TROY
I AM POSEIDON, GOD OF THE SEA. I CONTROL OCEANS, WINDS, WAVES, WEATHER, TRAVEL BY WATER, DEATH BY WATER, ETC. MY FUNCTION HERE IS TO "PROLOGUE" THE PLAY.
SET: LOOK BEHIND ME, THAT PILE OF RUBBLE, TROY.
TIME: DAY AFTER THE WAR – A DAY AS LONG AS THE REST OF THEIR LIVES FOR SOME, e.g. THAT MOB OF DOGS AND COWS YOU SEE DOWNSTAGE – PRISONERS OF WAR, LEFTOVER FEMALES. BRAINS BRIMMING. THEY'LL NEVER GET TO USE THEIR BRAINS AGAIN – SLAVES DON'T. THEY BARK AND WAIL – IGNORE IT.
STORY SO FAR. I BUILT TROY – IT WAS ME AND APOLLO DRAGGED THE STONES UP FROM THE BEACH, WE BUILT BOULEVARDS, WE DREAMED OF HEADLIGHTS GOING GHOSTING THROUGH THE FOG.

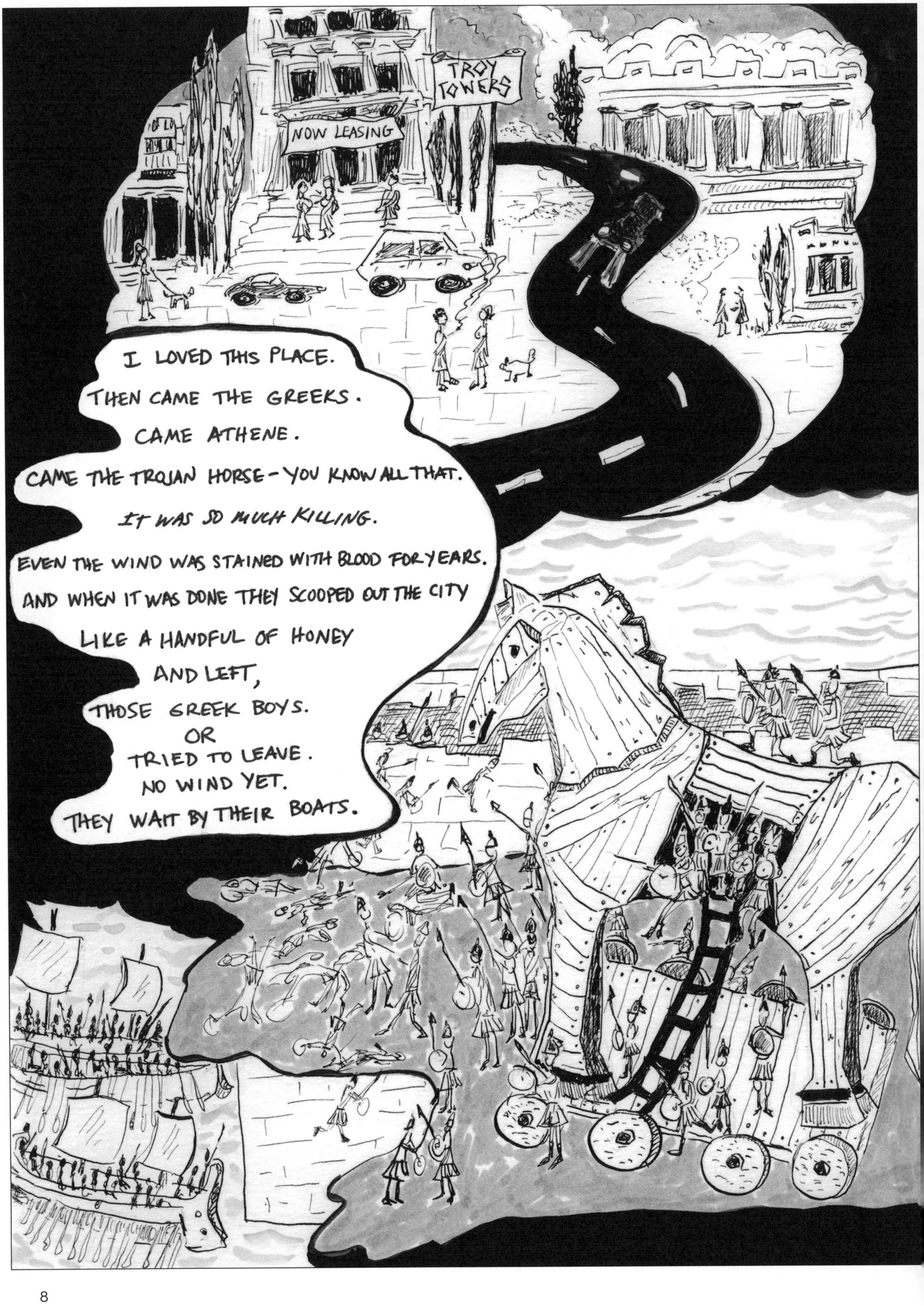

TROY TOWERS
NOW LEASING
I LOVED THIS PLACE.
THEN CAME THE GREEKS.
CAME ATHENE.
CAME THE TROJAN HORSE - YOU KNOW ALL THAT.
IT WAS SO MUCH KILLING.
EVEN THE WIND WAS STAINED WITH BLOOD FOR YEARS.
AND WHEN IT WAS DONE THEY SCOOPED OUT THE CITY
LIKE A HANDFUL OF HONEY
AND LEFT,
THOSE GREEK BOYS.
OR
TRIED TO LEAVE.
NO WIND YET.
THEY WAIT BY THEIR BOATS.

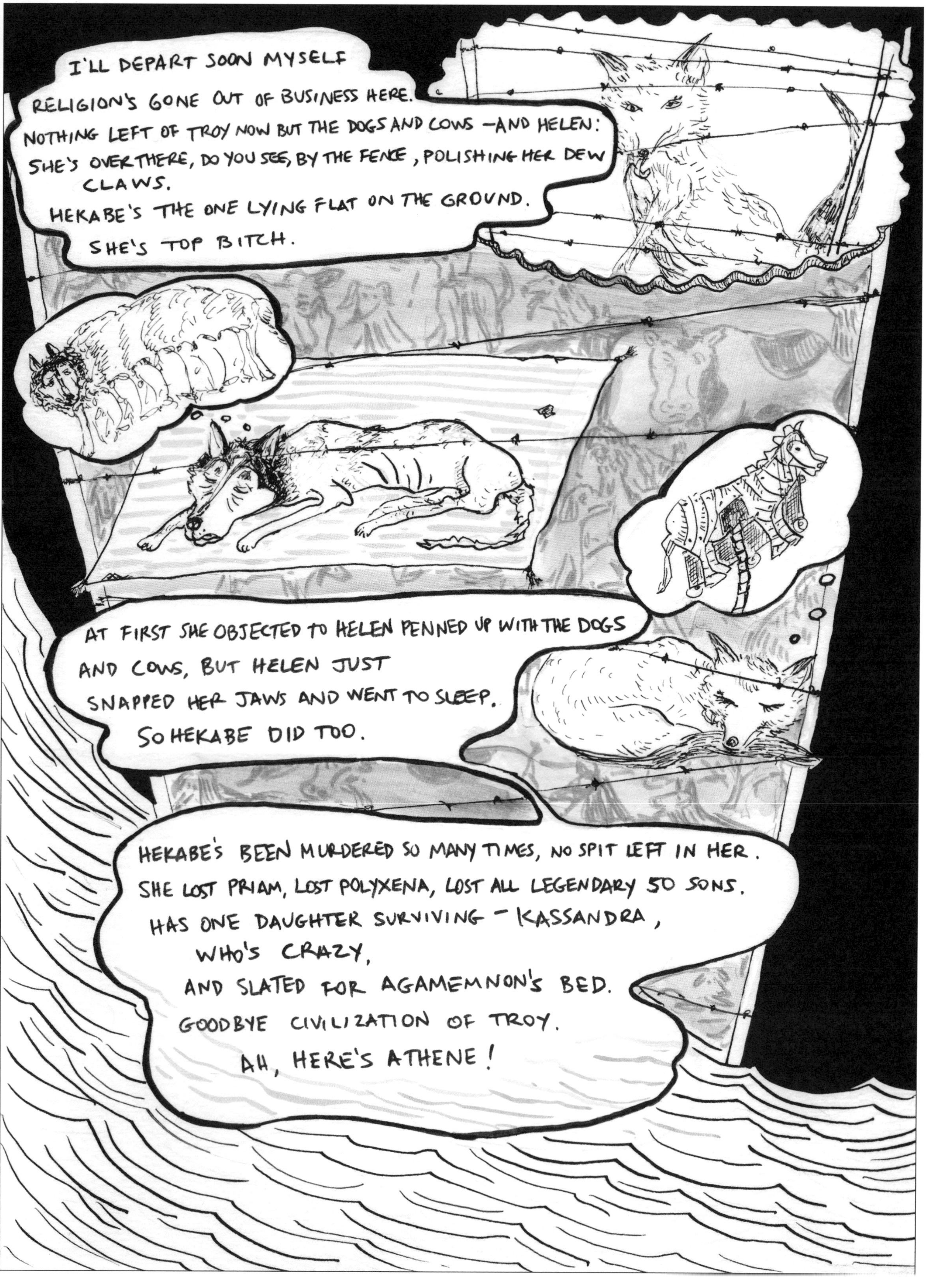
I'LL DEPART SOON MYSELF
RELIGION'S GONE OUT OF BUSINESS HERE.
NOTHING LEFT OF TROY NOW BUT THE DOGS AND COWS – AND HELEN:
SHE'S OVER THERE, DO YOU SEE, BY THE FENCE, POLISHING HER DEW CLAWS.
HEKABE'S THE ONE LYING FLAT ON THE GROUND.
SHE'S TOP BITCH.
AT FIRST SHE OBJECTED TO HELEN PENNED UP WITH THE DOGS AND COWS, BUT HELEN JUST SNAPPED HER JAWS AND WENT TO SLEEP.
SO HEKABE DID TOO.
HEKABE'S BEEN MURDERED SO MANY TIMES, NO SPIT LEFT IN HER.
SHE LOST PRIAM, LOST POLYXENA, LOST ALL LEGENDARY 50 SONS.
HAS ONE DAUGHTER SURVIVING – KASSANDRA, WHO'S CRAZY,
AND SLATED FOR AGAMEMNON'S BED.
GOODBYE CIVILIZATION OF TROY.
AH, HERE'S ATHENE!

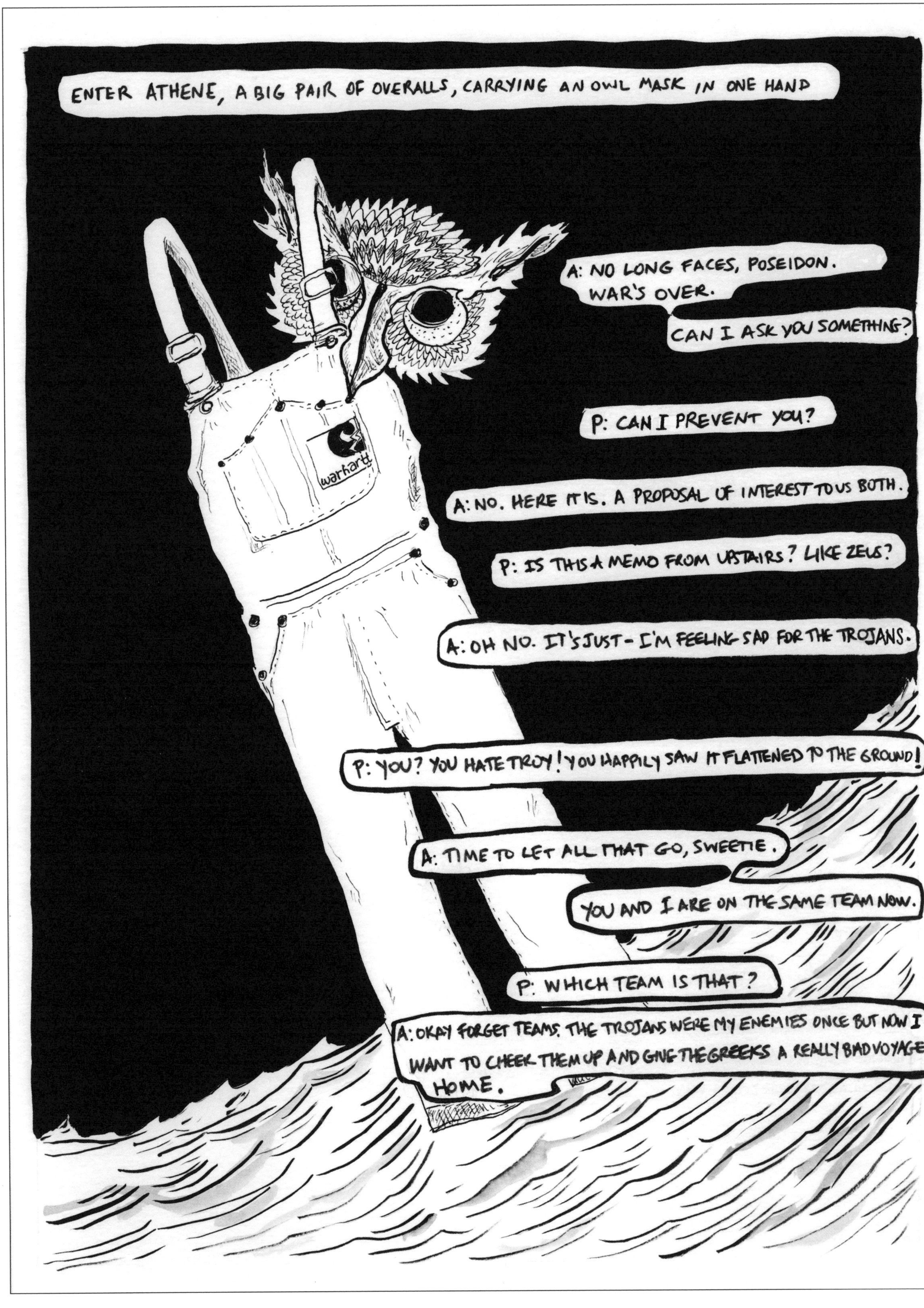
ENTER ATHENE, A BIG PAIR OF OVERALLS, CARRYING AN OWL MASK IN ONE HAND
A: NO LONG FACES, POSEIDON. WAR'S OVER.
CAN I ASK YOU SOMETHING?
P: CAN I PREVENT YOU?
A: NO. HERE IT IS. A PROPOSAL OF INTEREST TO US BOTH.
P: IS THIS A MEMO FROM UPSTAIRS? LIKE ZEUS?
A: OH NO. IT'S JUST - I'M FEELING SAD FOR THE TROJANS.
P: YOU? YOU HATE TROY! YOU HAPPILY SAW IT FLATTENED TO THE GROUND!
A: TIME TO LET ALL THAT GO, SWEETIE.
YOU AND I ARE ON THE SAME TEAM NOW.
P: WHICH TEAM IS THAT?
A: OKAY FORGET TEAMS. THE TROJANS WERE MY ENEMIES ONCE BUT NOW I WANT TO CHEER THEM UP AND GIVE THE GREEKS A REALLY BAD VOYAGE HOME.

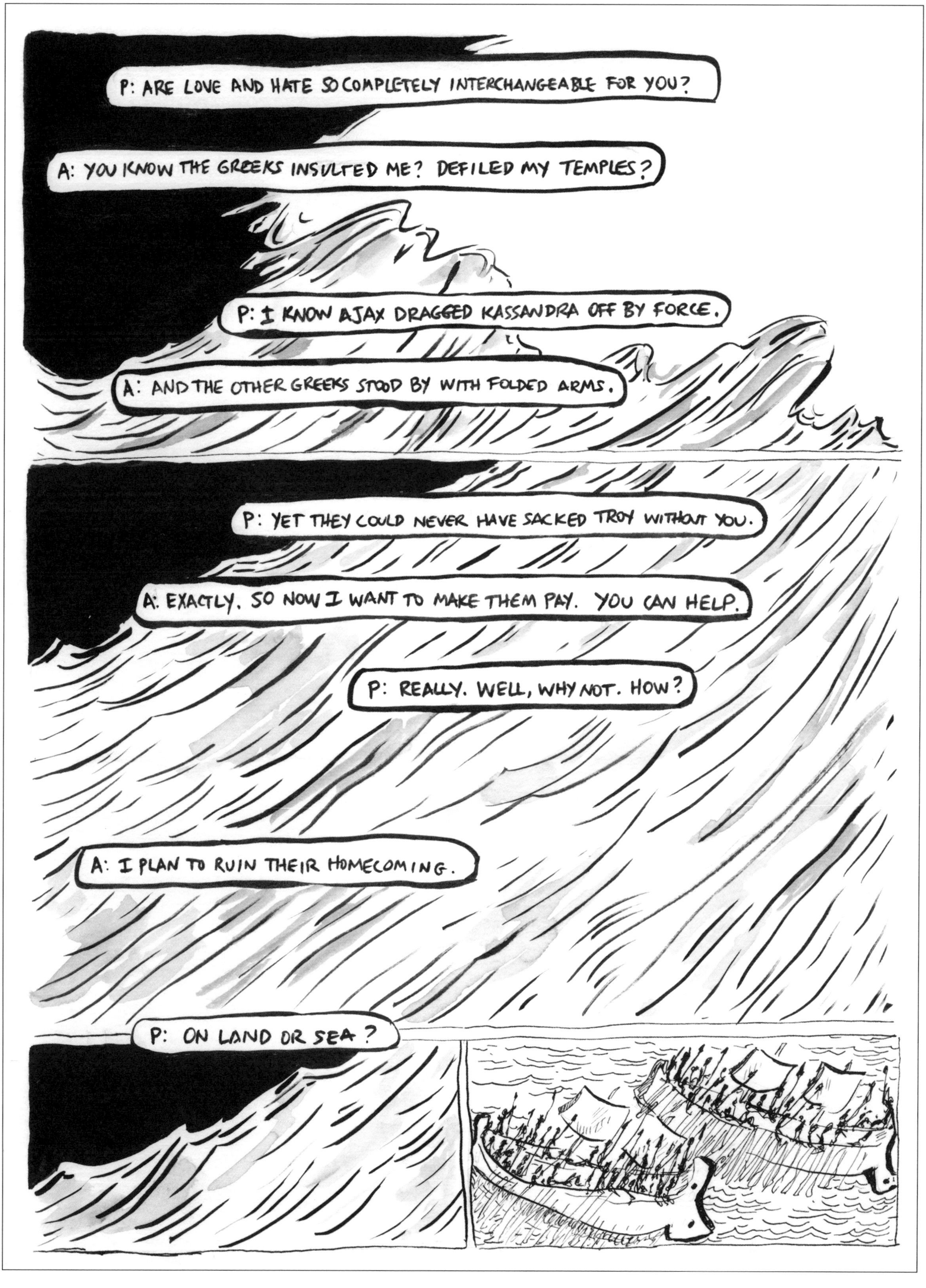
P: ARE LOVE AND HATE SO COMPLETELY INTERCHANGEABLE FOR YOU?
A: YOU KNOW THE GREEKS INSULTED ME? DEFILED MY TEMPLES?
P: I KNOW AJAX DRAGGED KASSANDRA OFF BY FORCE.
A: AND THE OTHER GREEKS STOOD BY WITH FOLDED ARMS.
P: YET THEY COULD NEVER HAVE SACKED TROY WITHOUT YOU.
A: EXACTLY. SO NOW I WANT TO MAKE THEM PAY. YOU CAN HELP.
P: REALLY. WELL, WHY NOT. HOW?
A: I PLAN TO RUIN THEIR HOMECOMING.
P: ON LAND OR SEA?

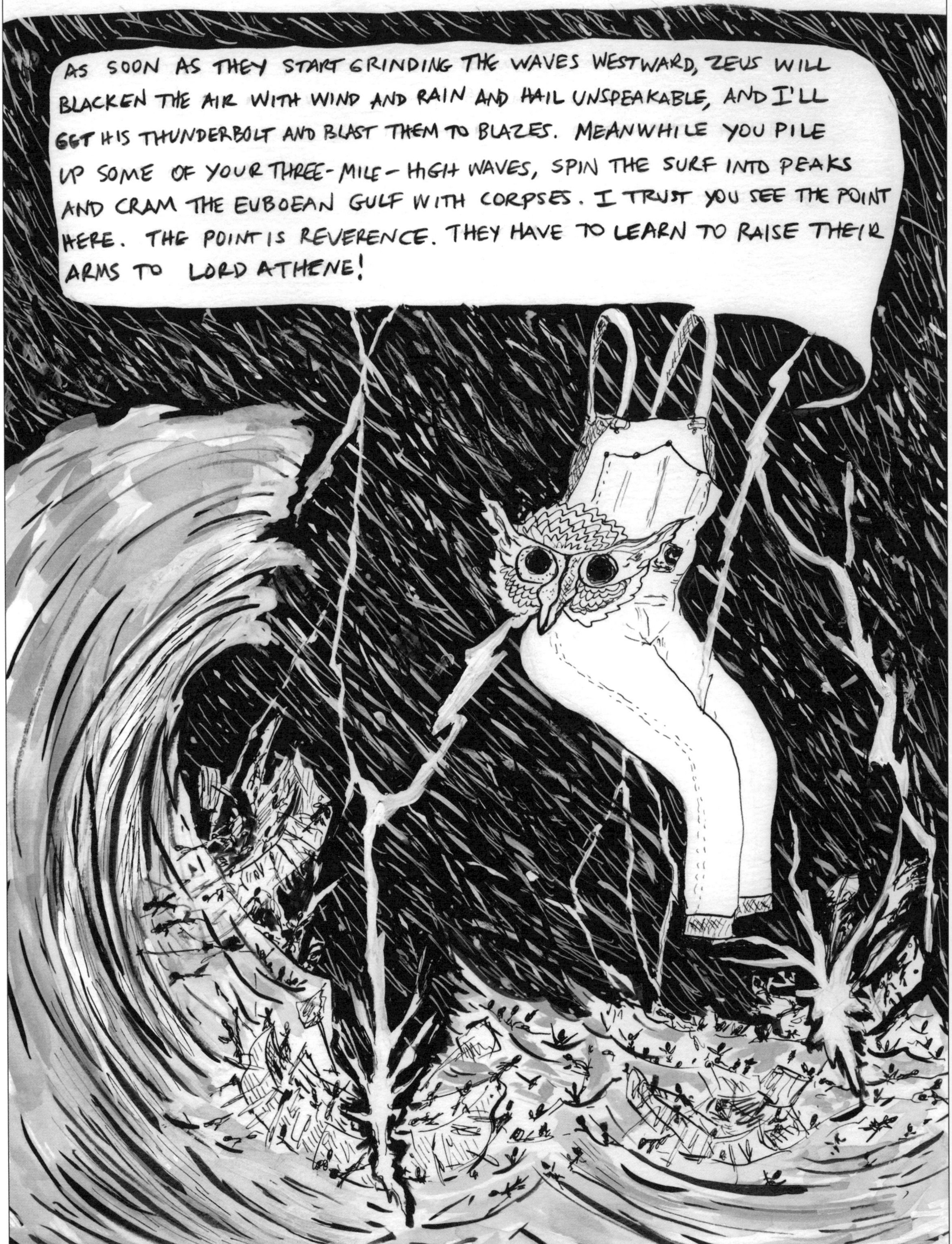
AS SOON AS THEY START GRINDING THE WAVES WESTWARD, ZEUS WILL BLACKEN THE AIR WITH WIND AND RAIN AND HAIL UNSPEAKABLE, AND I'LL GET HIS THUNDERBOLT AND BLAST THEM TO BLAZES. MEANWHILE YOU PILE UP SOME OF YOUR THREE-MILE-HIGH WAVES, SPIN THE SURF INTO PEAKS AND CRAM THE EUBOEAN GULF WITH CORPSES. I TRUST YOU SEE THE POINT HERE. THE POINT IS REVERENCE. THEY HAVE TO LEARN TO RAISE THEIR ARMS TO LORD ATHENE!

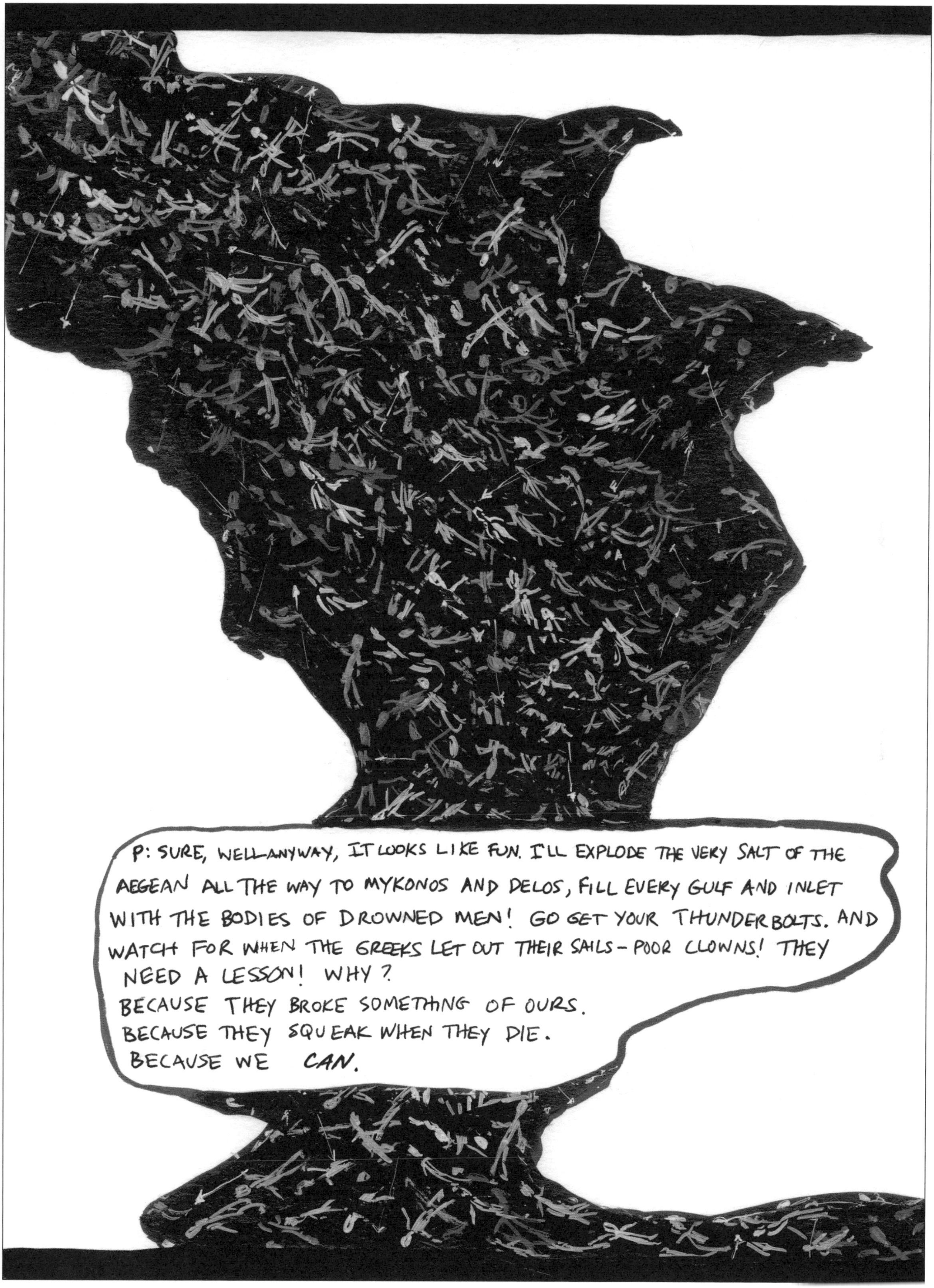
P: SURE, WELL ANYWAY, IT LOOKS LIKE FUN. I'LL EXPLODE THE VERY SALT OF THE AEGEAN ALL THE WAY TO MYKONOS AND DELOS, FILL EVERY GULF AND INLET WITH THE BODIES OF DROWNED MEN! GO GET YOUR THUNDERBOLTS. AND WATCH FOR WHEN THE GREEKS LET OUT THEIR SAILS - POOR CLOWNS! THEY NEED A LESSON! WHY?
BECAUSE THEY BROKE SOMETHING OF OURS.
BECAUSE THEY SQUEAK WHEN THEY DIE.
BECAUSE WE *CAN*.

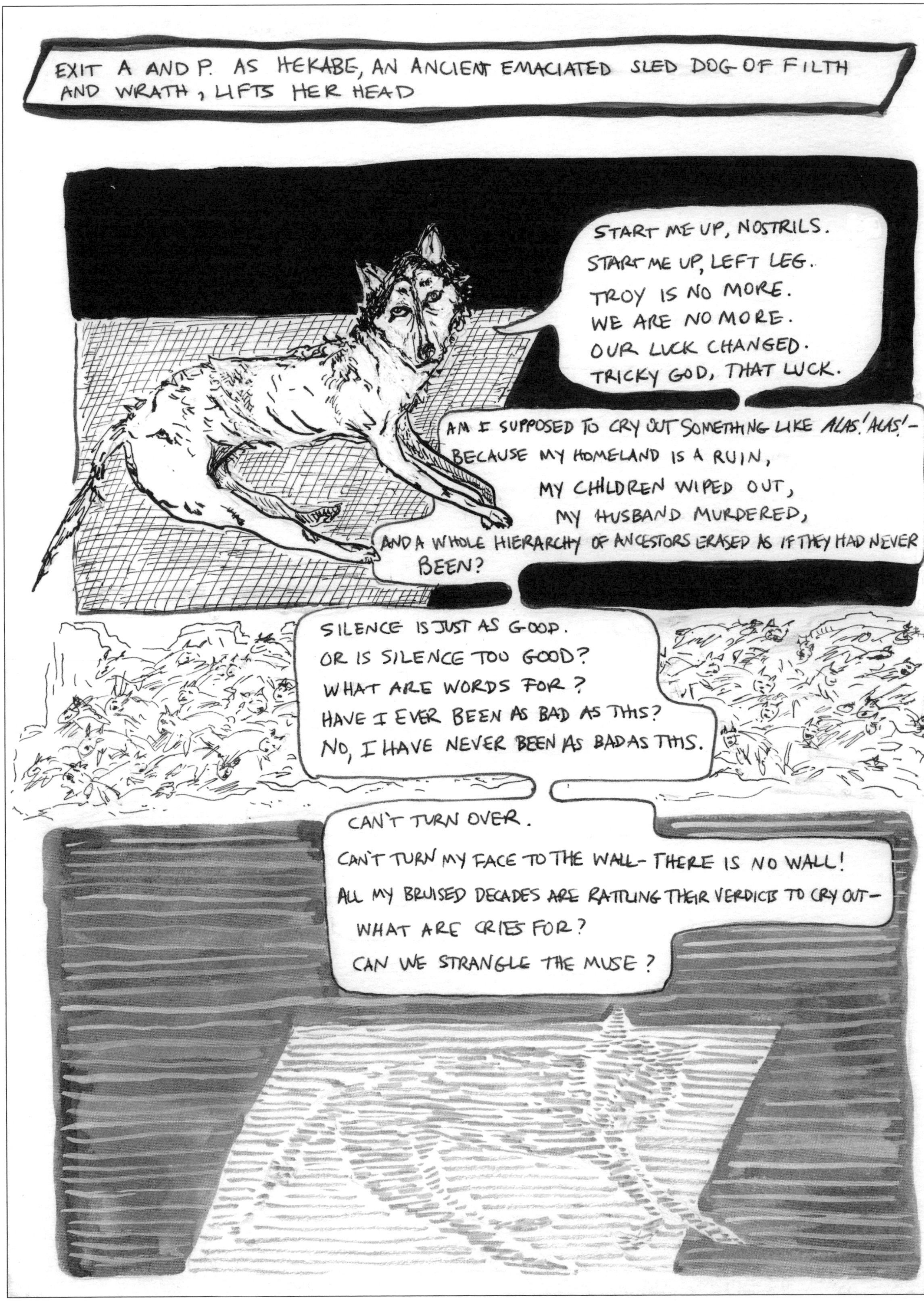
EXIT A AND P. AS HEKABE, AN ANCIENT EMACIATED SLED DOG OF FILTH AND WRATH, LIFTS HER HEAD
START ME UP, NOSTRILS. START ME UP, LEFT LEG. TROY IS NO MORE. WE ARE NO MORE. OUR LUCK CHANGED. TRICKY GOD, THAT LUCK.
AM I SUPPOSED TO CRY OUT SOMETHING LIKE ALAS! ALAS! – BECAUSE MY HOMELAND IS A RUIN, MY CHILDREN WIPED OUT, MY HUSBAND MURDERED, AND A WHOLE HIERARCHY OF ANCESTORS ERASED AS IF THEY HAD NEVER BEEN?
SILENCE IS JUST AS GOOD. OR IS SILENCE TOO GOOD? WHAT ARE WORDS FOR? HAVE I EVER BEEN AS BAD AS THIS? NO, I HAVE NEVER BEEN AS BAD AS THIS.
CAN'T TURN OVER. CAN'T TURN MY FACE TO THE WALL – THERE IS NO WALL! ALL MY BRUISED DECADES ARE RATTLING THEIR VERDICTS TO CRY OUT – WHAT ARE CRIES FOR? CAN WE STRANGLE THE MUSE?

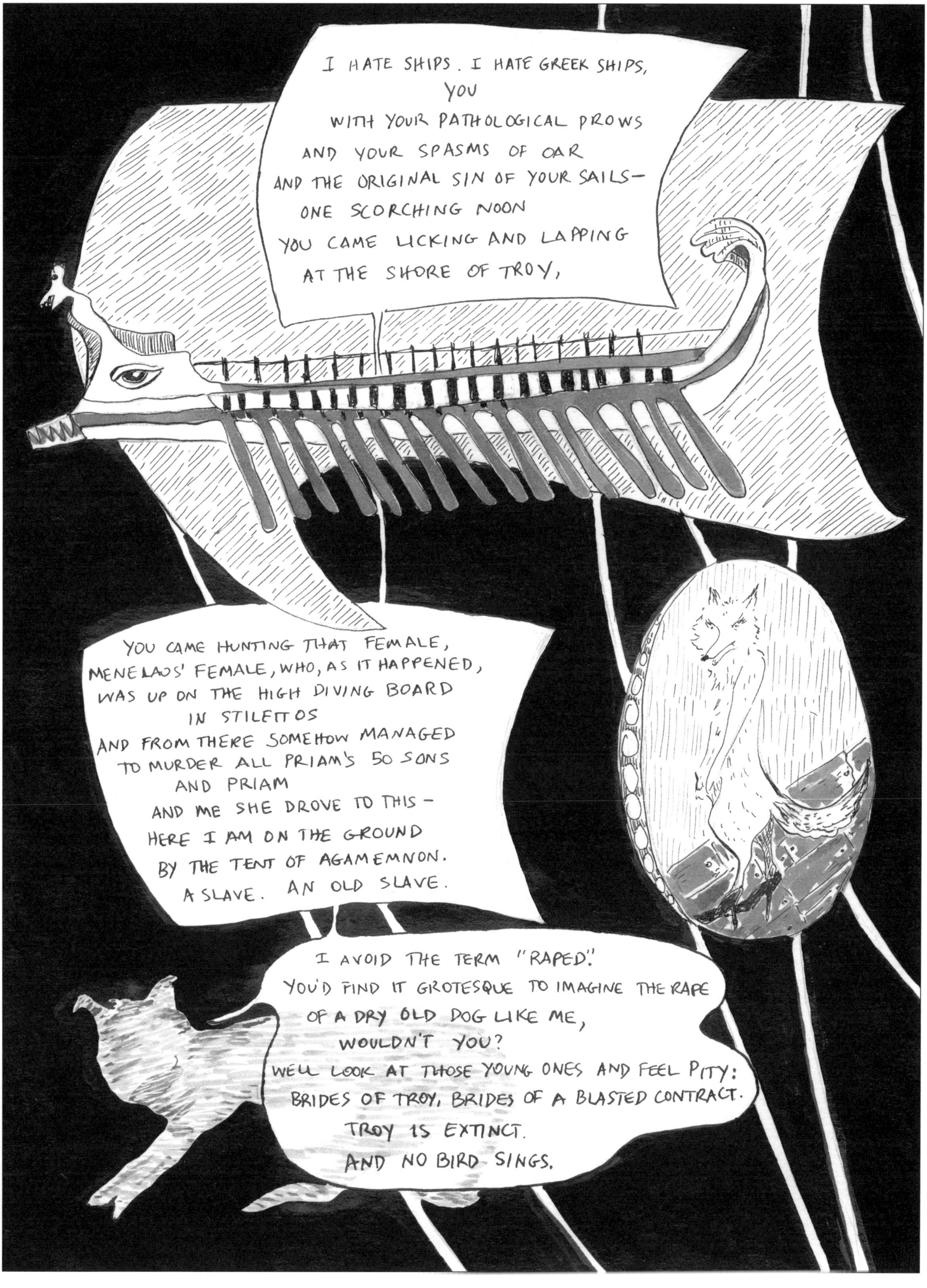
I HATE SHIPS. I HATE GREEK SHIPS,
YOU
WITH YOUR PATHOLOGICAL PROWS
AND YOUR SPASMS OF OAR
AND THE ORIGINAL SIN OF YOUR SAILS—
ONE SCORCHING NOON
YOU CAME LICKING AND LAPPING
AT THE SHORE OF TROY,
YOU CAME HUNTING THAT FEMALE,
MENELAOS' FEMALE, WHO, AS IT HAPPENED,
WAS UP ON THE HIGH DIVING BOARD
IN STILETTOS
AND FROM THERE SOMEHOW MANAGED
TO MURDER ALL PRIAM'S 50 SONS
AND PRIAM
AND ME SHE DROVE TO THIS –
HERE I AM ON THE GROUND
BY THE TENT OF AGAMEMNON.
A SLAVE. AN OLD SLAVE.
I AVOID THE TERM "RAPED".
YOU'D FIND IT GROTESQUE TO IMAGINE THE RAPE
OF A DRY OLD DOG LIKE ME,
WOULDN'T YOU?
WELL LOOK AT THOSE YOUNG ONES AND FEEL PITY:
BRIDES OF TROY, BRIDES OF A BLASTED CONTRACT.
TROY IS EXTINCT.
AND NO BIRD SINGS.

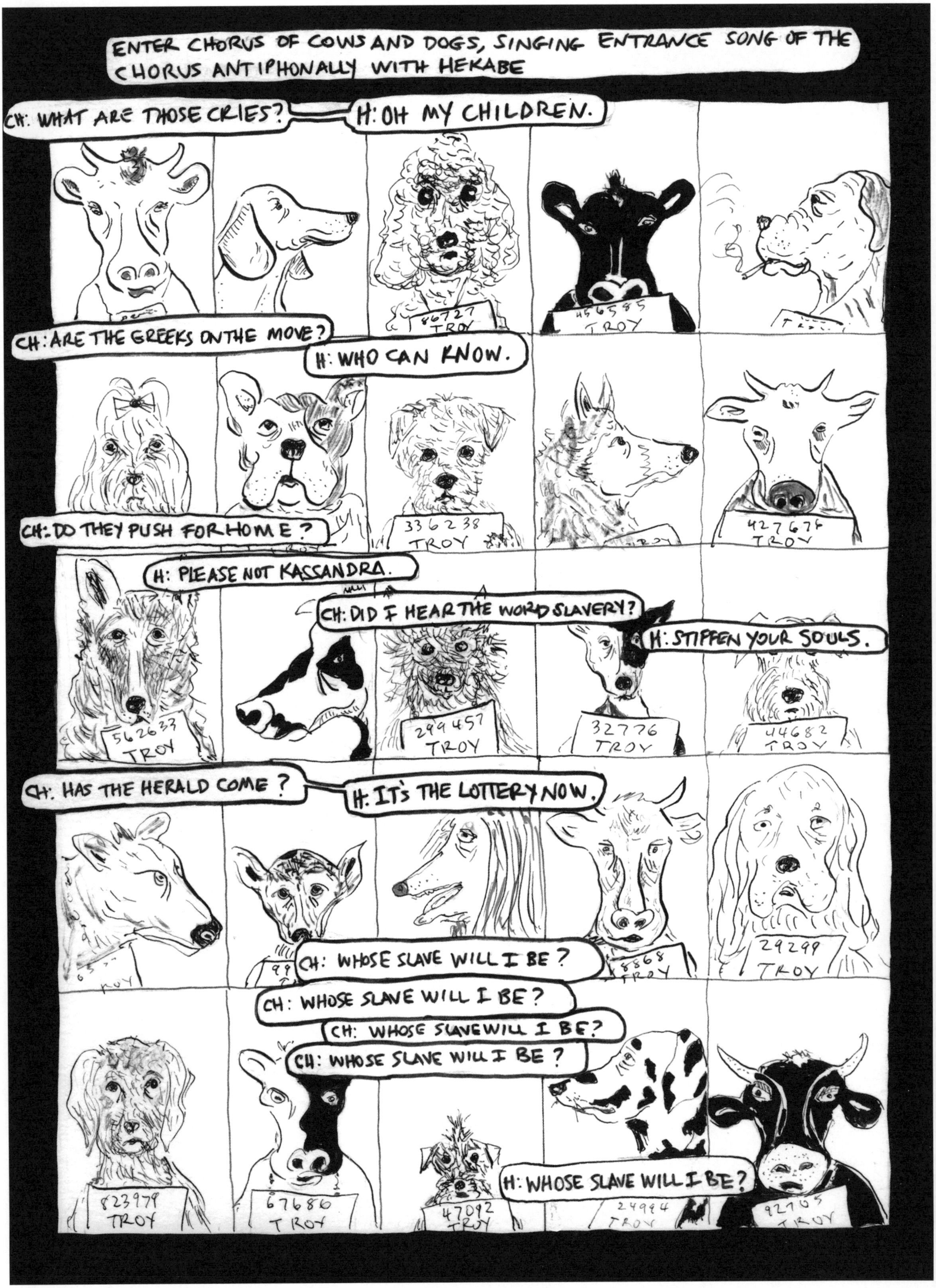
ENTER CHORUS OF COWS AND DOGS, SINGING ENTRANCE SONG OF THE CHORUS ANTIPHONALLY WITH HEKABE
CH: WHAT ARE THOSE CRIES?
H: OH MY CHILDREN.
86727 TROY
456585 TROY
CH: ARE THE GREEKS ON THE MOVE?
H: WHO CAN KNOW.
CH: DO THEY PUSH FOR HOME?
336238 TROY
427676 TROY
H: PLEASE NOT KASSANDRA.
CH: DID I HEAR THE WORD SLAVERY?
H: STIFFEN YOUR SOULS.
562633 TROY
299457 TROY
32776 TROY
44682 TROY
CH: HAS THE HERALD COME?
H: IT'S THE LOTTERY NOW.
CH: WHOSE SLAVE WILL I BE?
29299 TROY
CH: WHOSE SLAVE WILL I BE?
CH: WHOSE SLAVE WILL I BE?
CH: WHOSE SLAVE WILL I BE?
H: WHOSE SLAVE WILL I BE?
823979 TROY
67686 TROY
47092 TROY
24994 TROY
92705 TROY

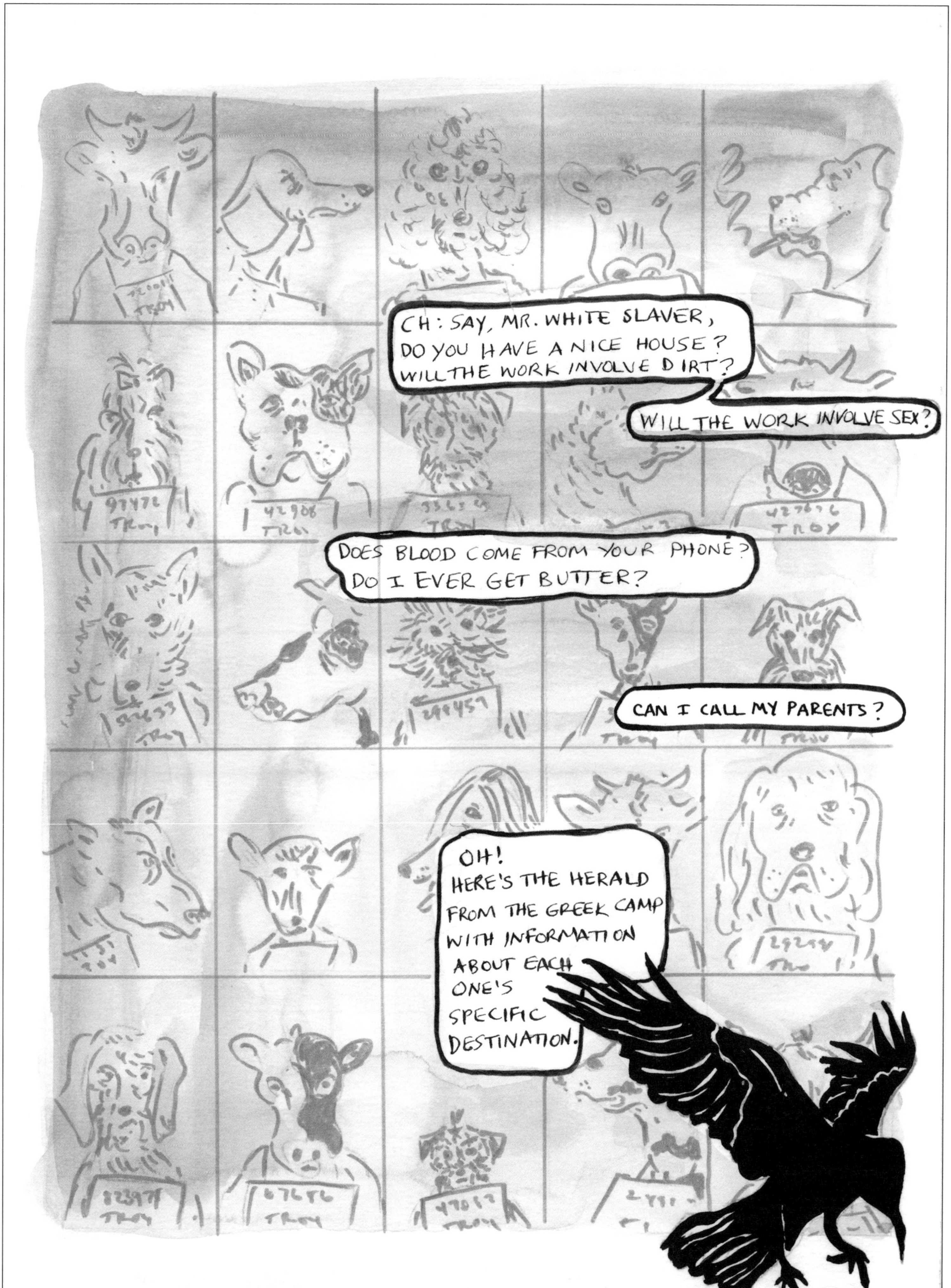
CH: SAY, MR. WHITE SLAVER, DO YOU HAVE A NICE HOUSE? WILL THE WORK INVOLVE DIRT?
WILL THE WORK INVOLVE SEX?
DOES BLOOD COME FROM YOUR PHONE? DO I EVER GET BUTTER?
CAN I CALL MY PARENTS?
OH! HERE'S THE HERALD FROM THE GREEK CAMP WITH INFORMATION ABOUT EACH ONE'S SPECIFIC DESTINATION.

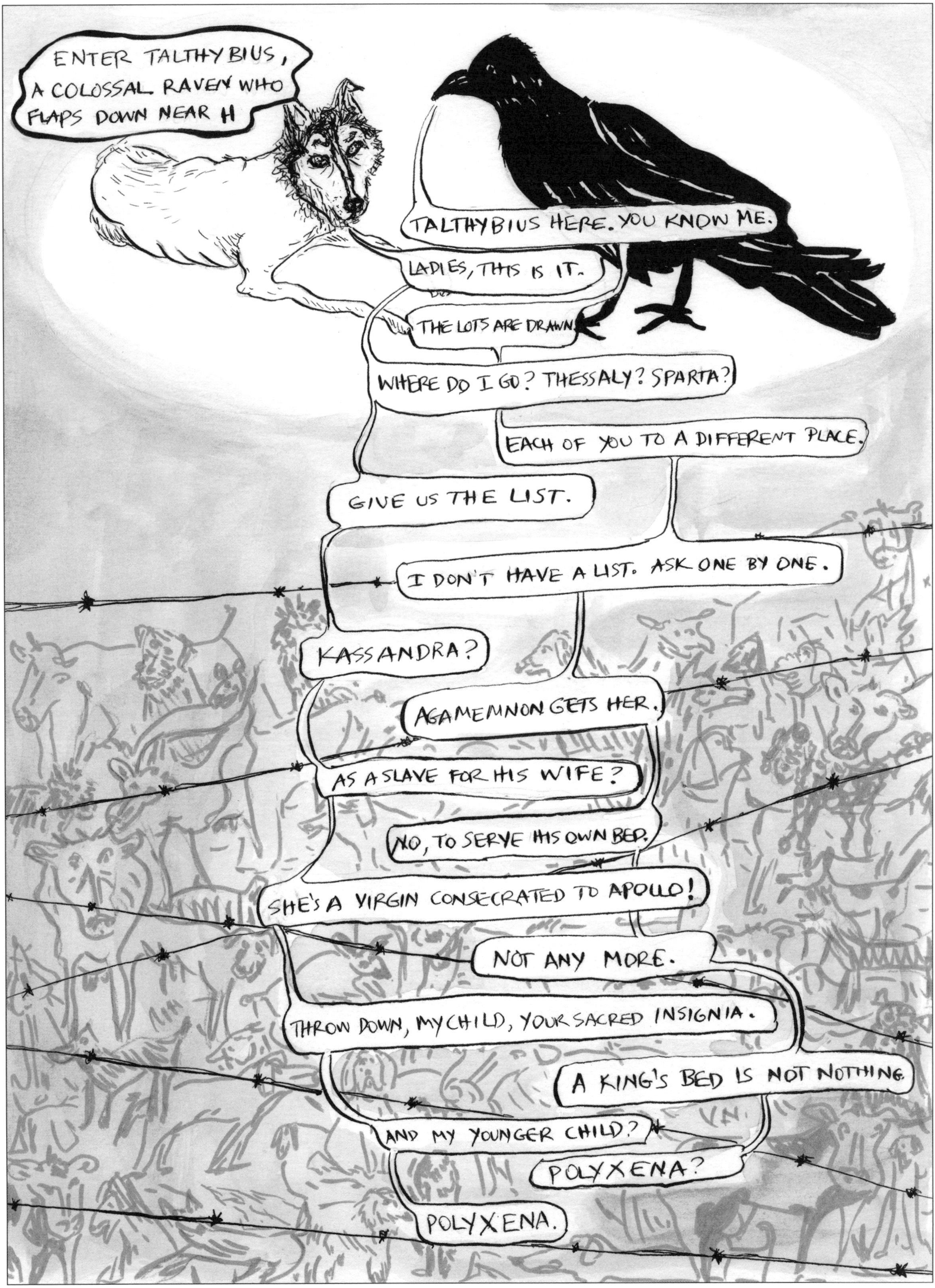
ENTER TALTHYBIUS, A COLOSSAL RAVEN WHO FLAPS DOWN NEAR H
TALTHYBIUS HERE. YOU KNOW ME.
LADIES, THIS IS IT.
THE LOTS ARE DRAWN.
WHERE DO I GO? THESSALY? SPARTA?
EACH OF YOU TO A DIFFERENT PLACE.
GIVE US THE LIST.
I DON'T HAVE A LIST. ASK ONE BY ONE.
KASSANDRA?
AGAMEMNON GETS HER.
AS A SLAVE FOR HIS WIFE?
NO, TO SERVE HIS OWN BED.
SHE'S A VIRGIN CONSECRATED TO APOLLO!
NOT ANY MORE.
THROW DOWN, MY CHILD, YOUR SACRED INSIGNIA.
A KING'S BED IS NOT NOTHING.
AND MY YOUNGER CHILD?
POLYXENA?
POLYXENA.

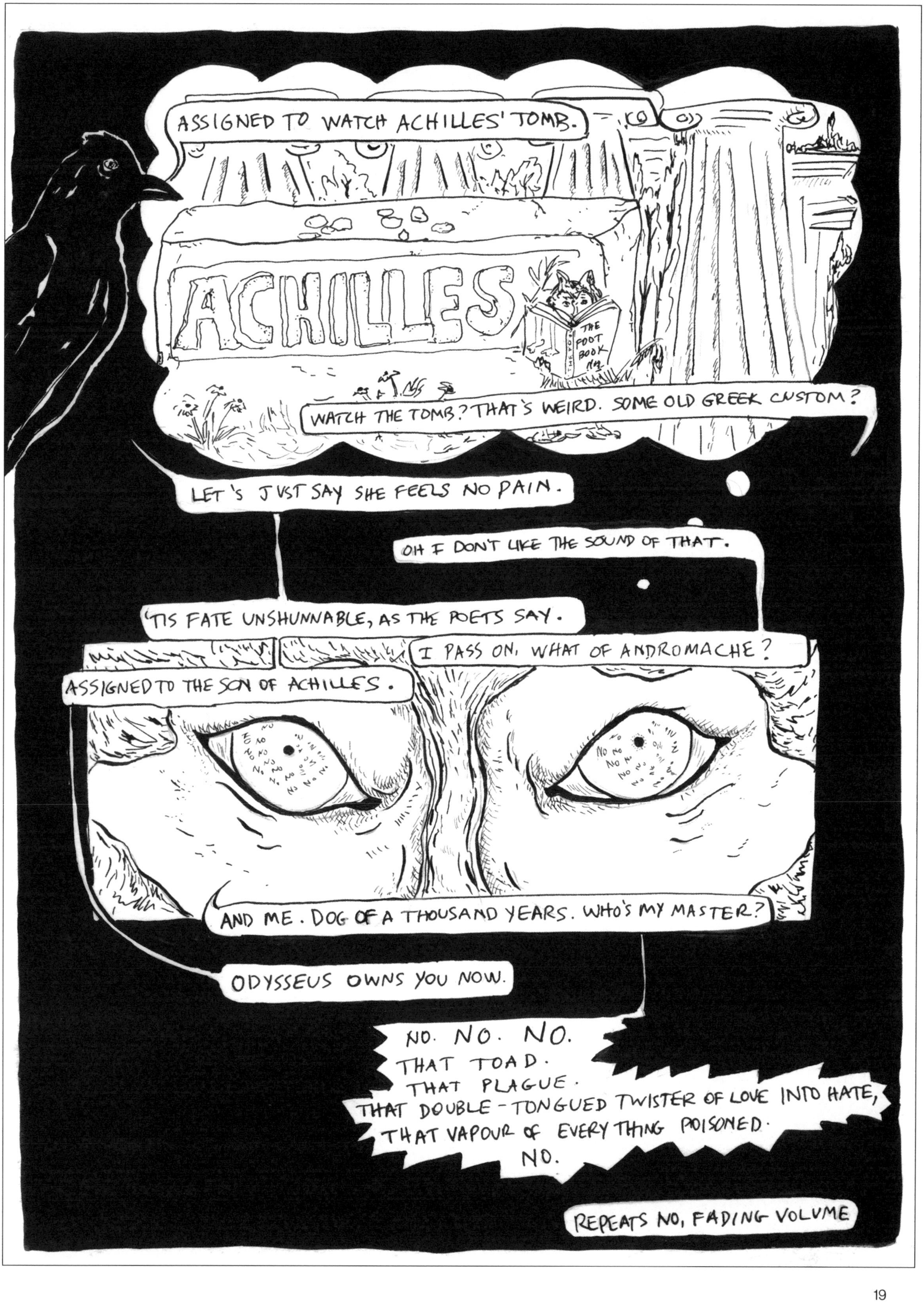

ASSIGNED TO WATCH ACHILLES' TOMB.
ACHILLES
THE FOOT BOOK
WATCH THE TOMB? THAT'S WEIRD. SOME OLD GREEK CUSTOM?
LET'S JUST SAY SHE FEELS NO PAIN.
OH I DON'T LIKE THE SOUND OF THAT.
'TIS FATE UNSHUNNABLE, AS THE POETS SAY.
I PASS ON. WHAT OF ANDROMACHE?
ASSIGNED TO THE SON OF ACHILLES.
AND ME. DOG OF A THOUSAND YEARS. WHO'S MY MASTER?
ODYSSEUS OWNS YOU NOW.
NO. NO. NO. THAT TOAD. THAT PLAGUE. THAT DOUBLE-TONGUED TWISTER OF LOVE INTO HATE, THAT VAPOUR OF EVERY THING POISONED. NO.
REPEATS NO, FADING VOLUME

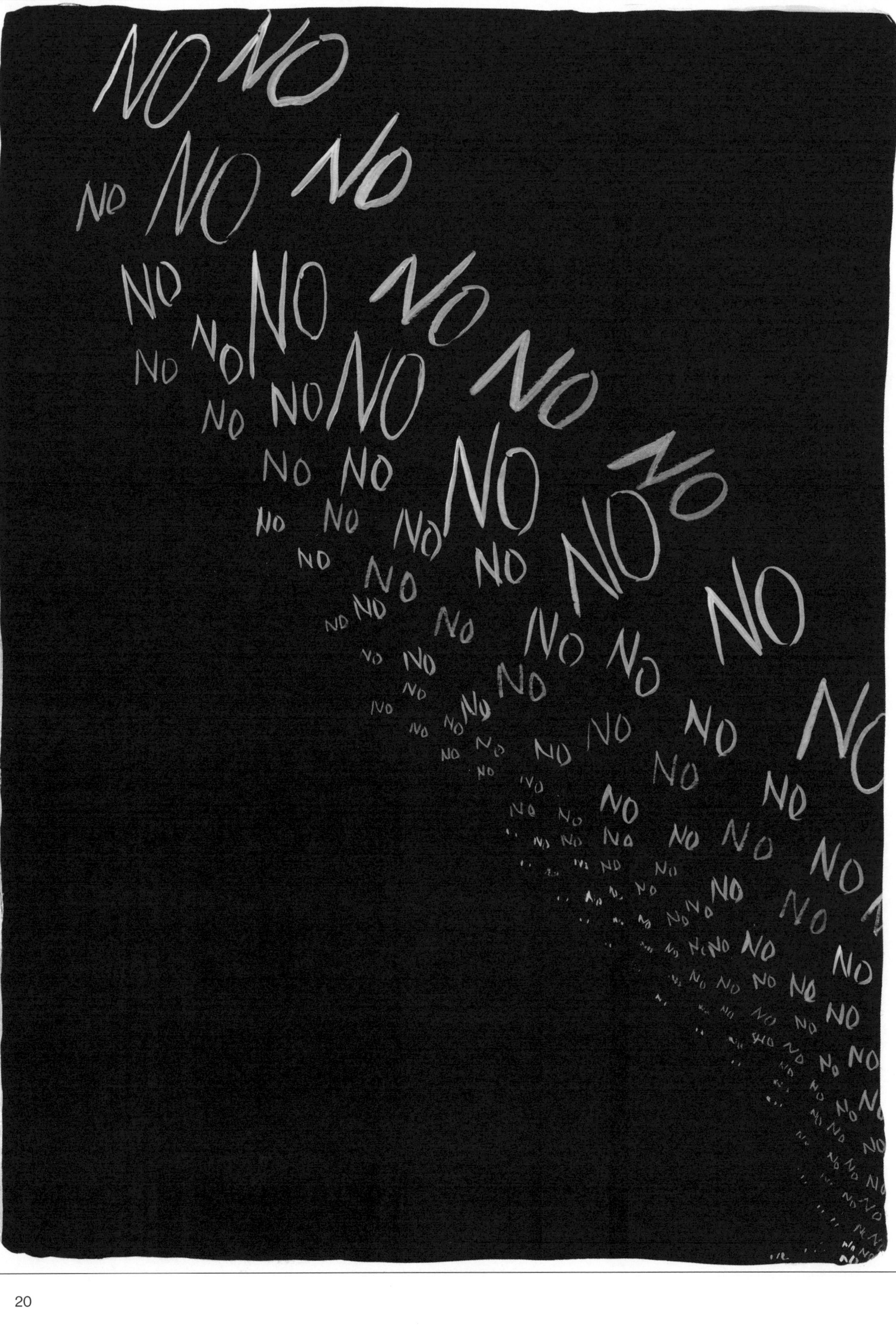
NO NO
NO NO NO
NO NO NO
NO NO NO NO
NO NO NO
NO NO NO NO
NO NO NO NO
NO NO NO NO
NO NO NO NO NO
NO NO NO NO NO
NO NO NO NO NO
NO NO NO NO NO

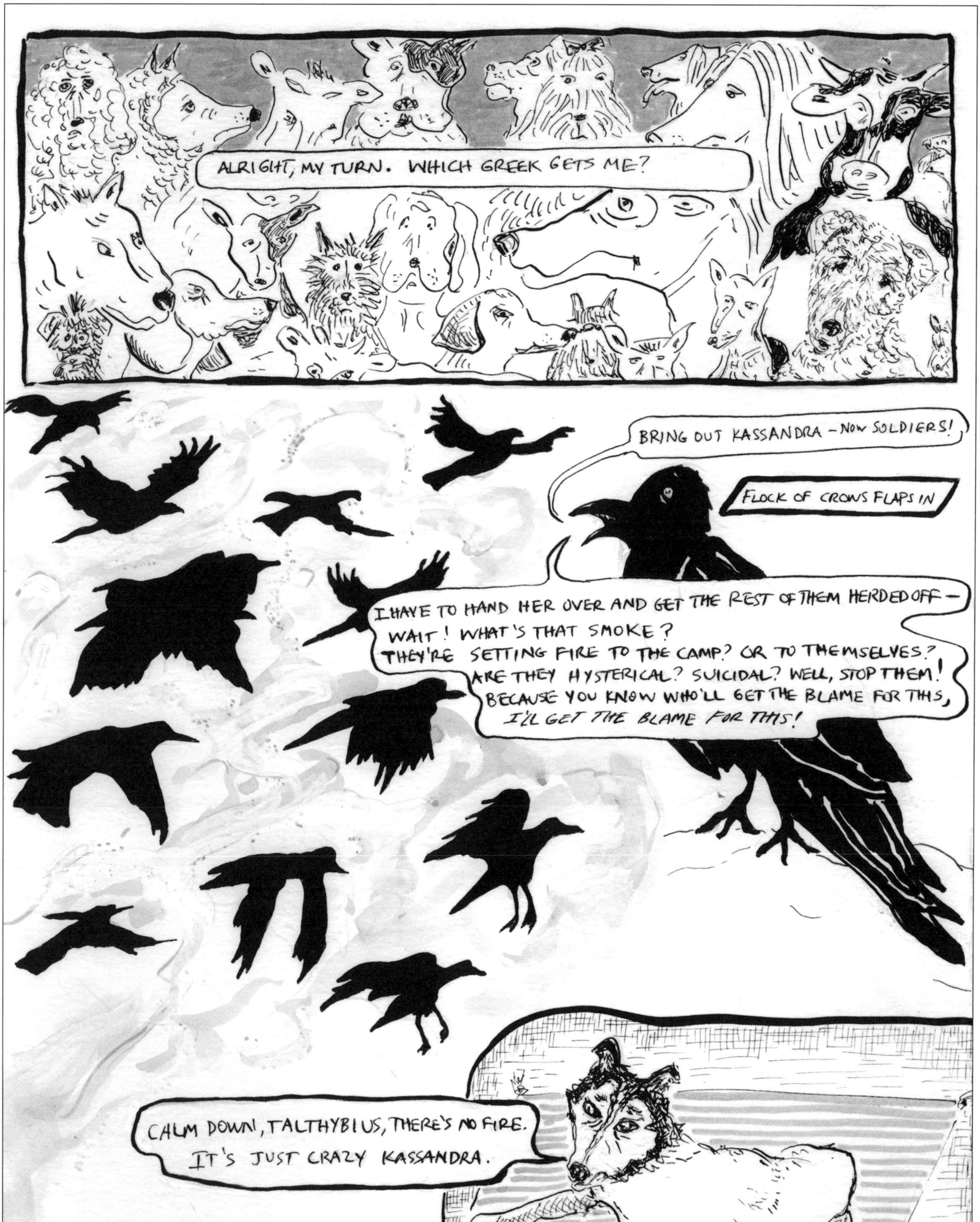
ALRIGHT, MY TURN. WHICH GREEK GETS ME?
BRING OUT KASSANDRA – NOW SOLDIERS!
FLOCK OF CROWS FLAPS IN
I HAVE TO HAND HER OVER AND GET THE REST OF THEM HERDED OFF – WAIT! WHAT'S THAT SMOKE? THEY'RE SETTING FIRE TO THE CAMP? OR TO THEMSELVES? ARE THEY HYSTERICAL? SUICIDAL? WELL, STOP THEM! BECAUSE YOU KNOW WHO'LL GET THE BLAME FOR THIS, I'LL GET THE BLAME FOR THIS!
CALM DOWN!, TALTHYBIUS, THERE'S NO FIRE. IT'S JUST CRAZY KASSANDRA.

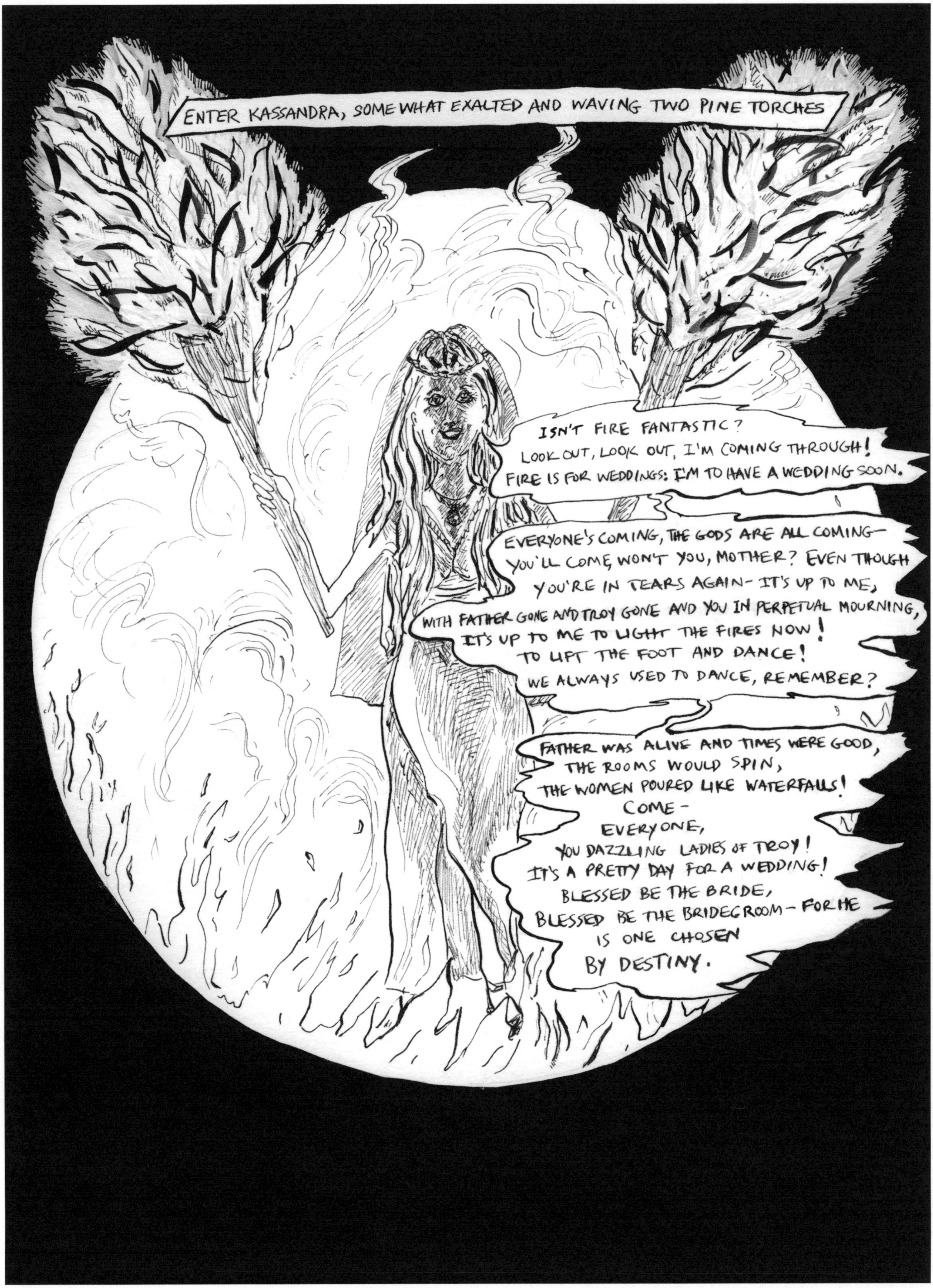
ENTER KASSANDRA, SOMEWHAT EXALTED AND WAVING TWO PINE TORCHES
ISN'T FIRE FANTASTIC? LOOK OUT, LOOK OUT, I'M COMING THROUGH! FIRE IS FOR WEDDINGS: I'M TO HAVE A WEDDING SOON.
EVERYONE'S COMING, THE GODS ARE ALL COMING- YOU'LL COME, WON'T YOU, MOTHER? EVEN THOUGH YOU'RE IN TEARS AGAIN- IT'S UP TO ME, WITH FATHER GONE AND TROY GONE AND YOU IN PERPETUAL MOURNING, IT'S UP TO ME TO LIGHT THE FIRES NOW! TO LIFT THE FOOT AND DANCE! WE ALWAYS USED TO DANCE, REMEMBER?
FATHER WAS ALIVE AND TIMES WERE GOOD, THE ROOMS WOULD SPIN, THE WOMEN POURED LIKE WATERFALLS! COME- EVERYONE, YOU DAZZLING LADIES OF TROY! IT'S A PRETTY DAY FOR A WEDDING! BLESSED BE THE BRIDE, BLESSED BE THE BRIDEGROOM- FOR HE IS ONE CHOSEN BY DESTINY.

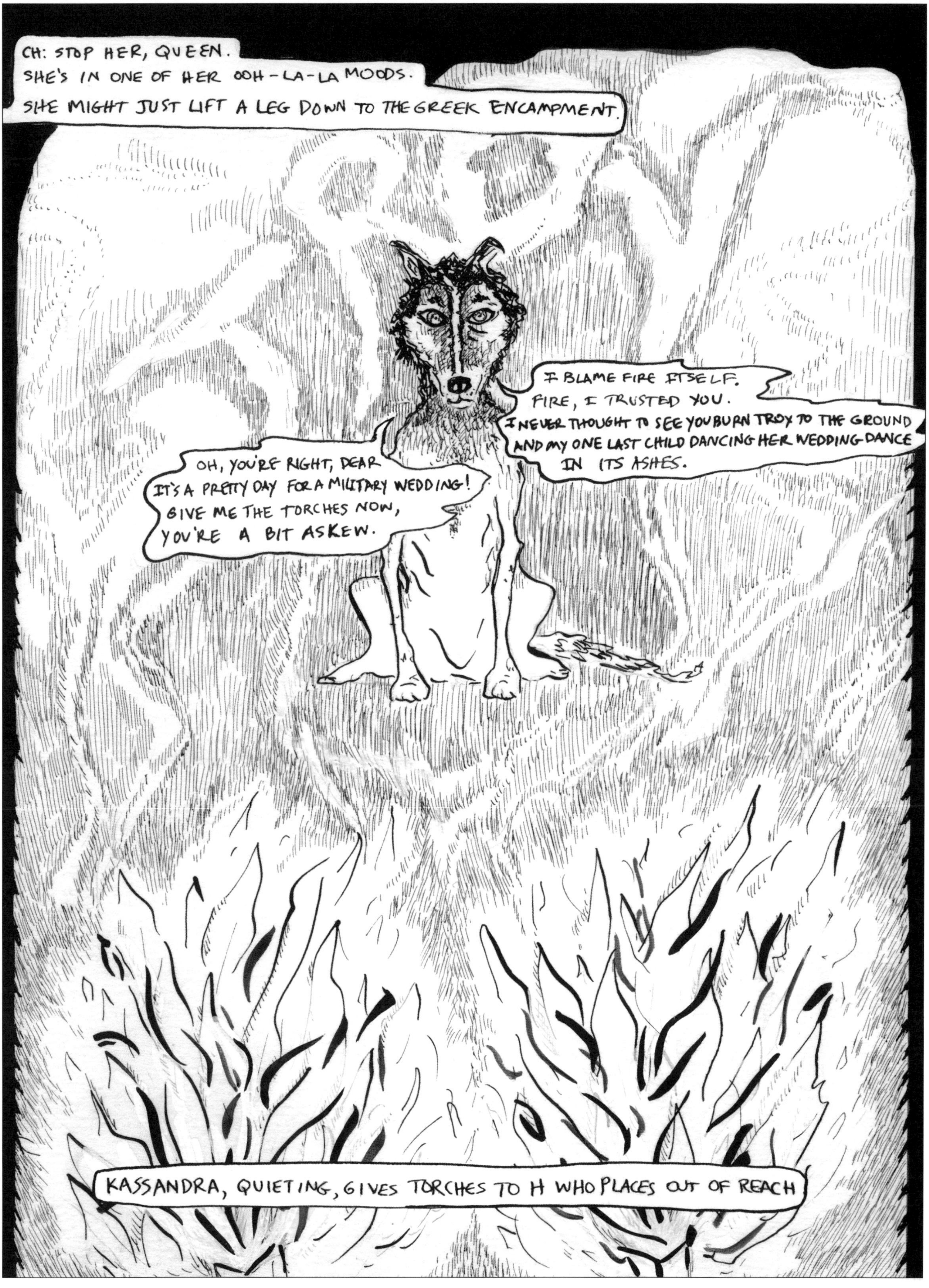
CH: STOP HER, QUEEN.
SHE'S IN ONE OF HER OOH-LA-LA MOODS.
SHE MIGHT JUST LIFT A LEG DOWN TO THE GREEK ENCAMPMENT.
I BLAME FIRE ITSELF. FIRE, I TRUSTED YOU. I NEVER THOUGHT TO SEE YOU BURN TROY TO THE GROUND AND MY ONE LAST CHILD DANCING HER WEDDING DANCE IN ITS ASHES.
OH, YOU'RE RIGHT, DEAR IT'S A PRETTY DAY FOR A MILITARY WEDDING! GIVE ME THE TORCHES NOW, YOU'RE A BIT ASKEW.
KASSANDRA, QUIETING, GIVES TORCHES TO H WHO PLACES OUT OF REACH

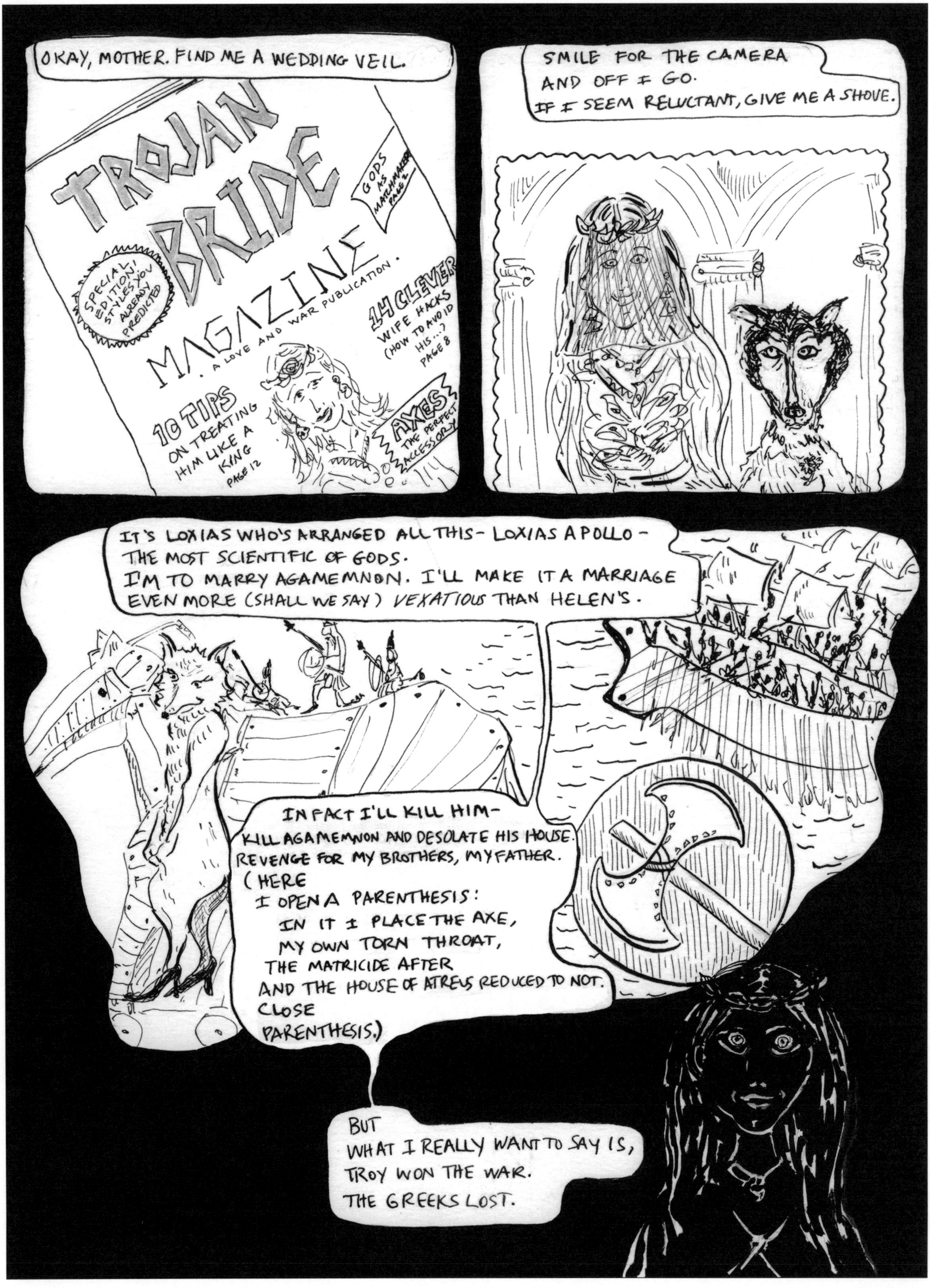
OKAY, MOTHER. FIND ME A WEDDING VEIL.
TROJAN BRIDE MAGAZINE
A LOVE AND WAR PUBLICATION.
SPECIAL EDITION! STYLES YOU ALREADY PREDICTED
GODS AS MATCHMAKERS PAGE 2
14 CLEVER WIFE HACKS (HOW TO AVOID HIS...?) PAGE 8
10 TIPS ON TREATING HIM LIKE A KING PAGE 12
AXES THE PERFECT ACCESSORY
SMILE FOR THE CAMERA AND OFF I GO. IF I SEEM RELUCTANT, GIVE ME A SHOVE.
IT'S LOXIAS WHO'S ARRANGED ALL THIS – LOXIAS APOLLO – THE MOST SCIENTIFIC OF GODS. I'M TO MARRY AGAMEMNON. I'LL MAKE IT A MARRIAGE EVEN MORE (SHALL WE SAY) *VEXATIOUS* THAN HELEN'S.
IN FACT I'LL KILL HIM – KILL AGAMEMNON AND DESOLATE HIS HOUSE. REVENGE FOR MY BROTHERS, MY FATHER. (HERE I OPEN A PARENTHESIS: IN IT I PLACE THE AXE, MY OWN TORN THROAT, THE MATRICIDE AFTER AND THE HOUSE OF ATREUS REDUCED TO NOT. CLOSE PARENTHESIS.)
BUT WHAT I REALLY WANT TO SAY IS, TROY WON THE WAR. THE GREEKS LOST.

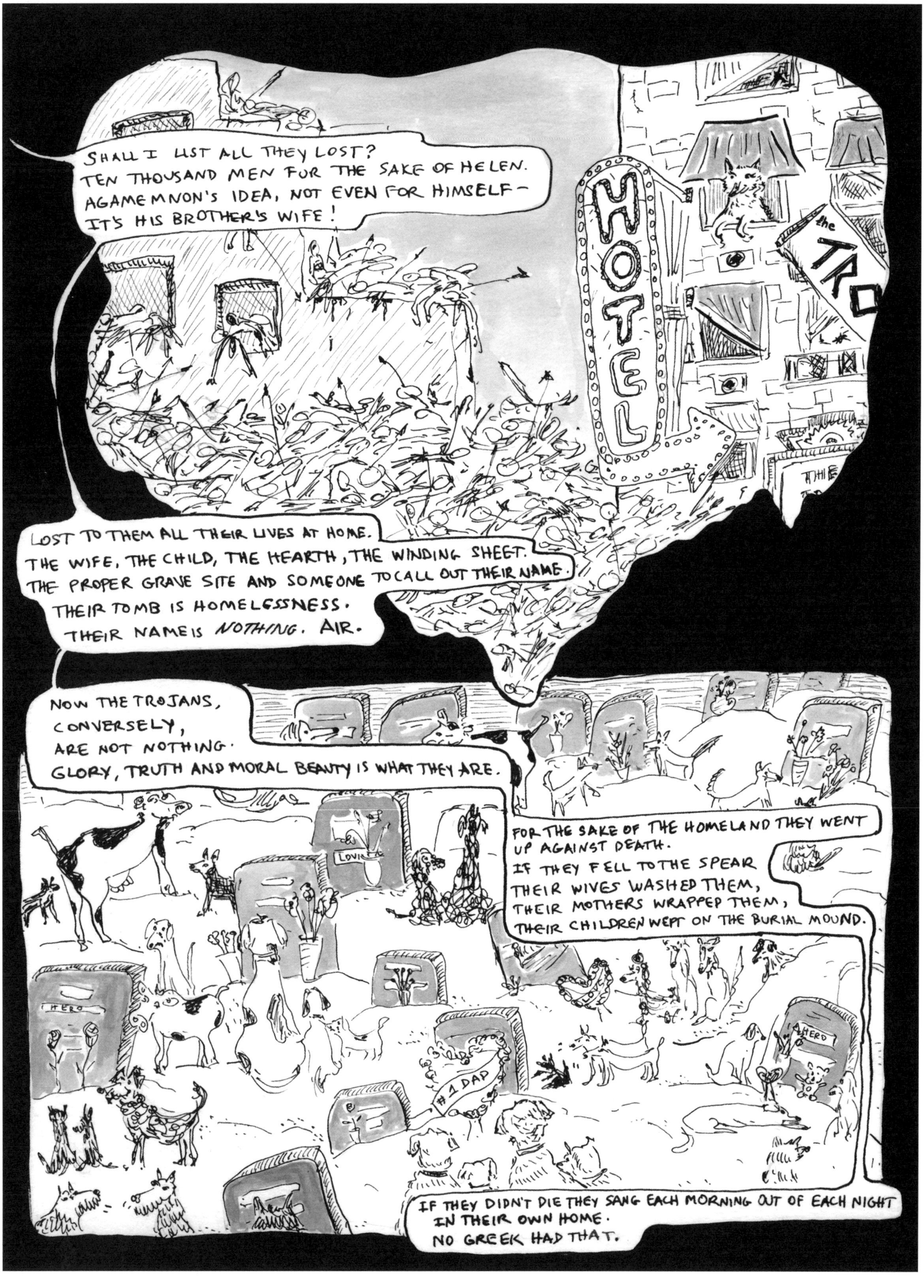
SHALL I LIST ALL THEY LOST?
TEN THOUSAND MEN FOR THE SAKE OF HELEN.
AGAMEMNON'S IDEA, NOT EVEN FOR HIMSELF—
IT'S HIS BROTHER'S WIFE!
HOTEL
the TRO
LOST TO THEM ALL THEIR LIVES AT HOME.
THE WIFE, THE CHILD, THE HEARTH, THE WINDING SHEET.
THE PROPER GRAVE SITE AND SOMEONE TO CALL OUT THEIR NAME.
THEIR TOMB IS HOMELESSNESS.
THEIR NAME IS *NOTHING*. AIR.
NOW THE TROJANS,
CONVERSELY,
ARE NOT NOTHING.
GLORY, TRUTH AND MORAL BEAUTY IS WHAT THEY ARE.
FOR THE SAKE OF THE HOMELAND THEY WENT UP AGAINST DEATH.
IF THEY FELL TO THE SPEAR
THEIR WIVES WASHED THEM,
THEIR MOTHERS WRAPPED THEM,
THEIR CHILDREN WEPT ON THE BURIAL MOUND.
HERO
HERO
#1 DAD
IF THEY DIDN'T DIE THEY SANG EACH MORNING OUT OF EACH NIGHT
IN THEIR OWN HOME.
NO GREEK HAD THAT.

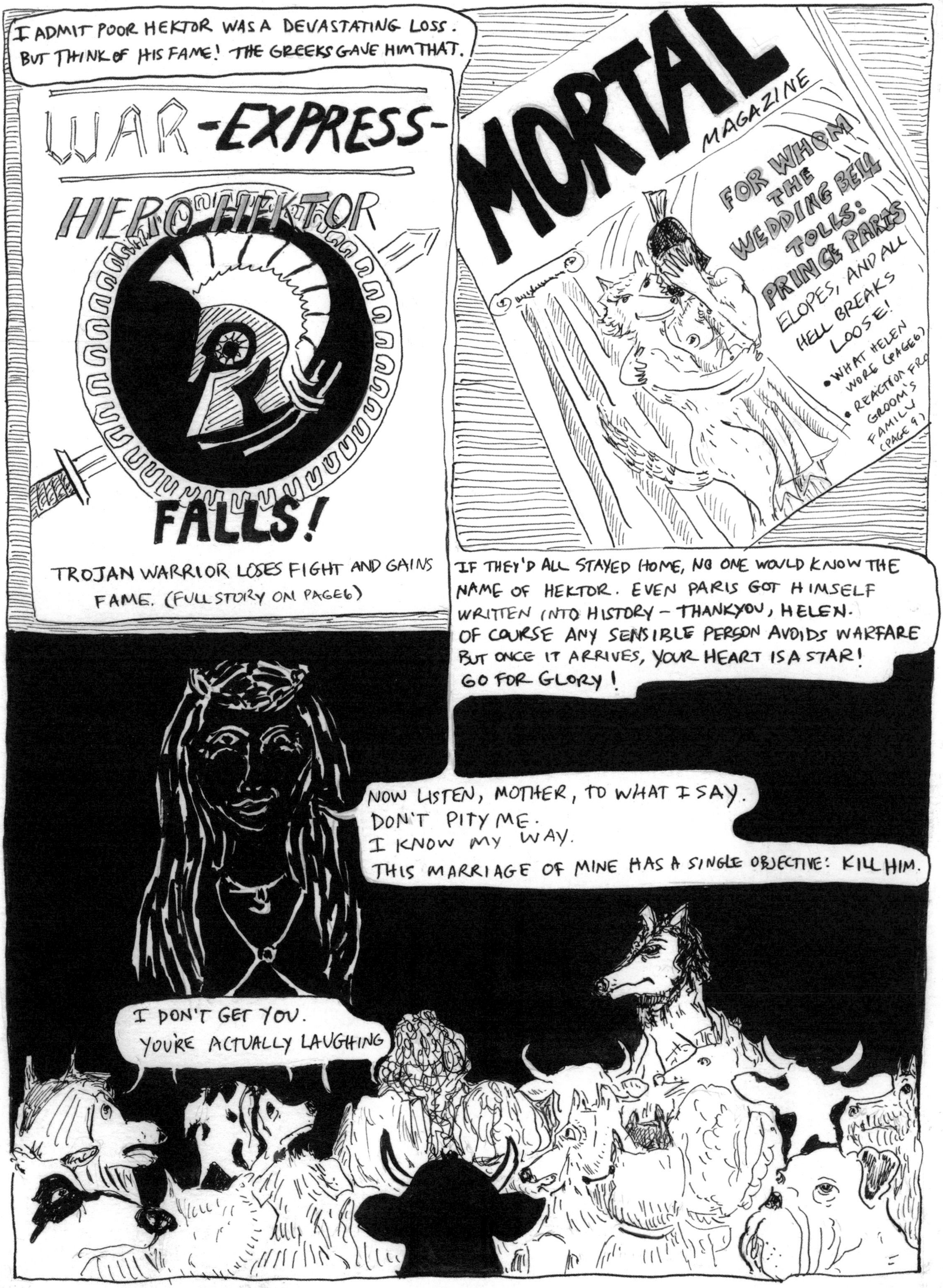
I ADMIT POOR HEKTOR WAS A DEVASTATING LOSS. BUT THINK OF HIS FAME! THE GREEKS GAVE HIM THAT.
WAR -EXPRESS-
HERO HEKTOR
FALLS!
TROJAN WARRIOR LOSES FIGHT AND GAINS FAME. (FULL STORY ON PAGE 6)
MORTAL
MAGAZINE
FOR WHOM THE WEDDING BELL TOLLS: PRINCE PARIS ELOPES, AND ALL HELL BREAKS LOOSE!
• WHAT HELEN WORE (PAGE 6)
• REACTION FRO GROOM'S FAMILY (PAGE 9)
IF THEY'D ALL STAYED HOME, NO ONE WOULD KNOW THE NAME OF HEKTOR. EVEN PARIS GOT HIMSELF WRITTEN INTO HISTORY – THANKYOU, HELEN. OF COURSE ANY SENSIBLE PERSON AVOIDS WARFARE BUT ONCE IT ARRIVES, YOUR HEART IS A STAR! GO FOR GLORY!
NOW LISTEN, MOTHER, TO WHAT I SAY. DON'T PITY ME. I KNOW MY WAY. THIS MARRIAGE OF MINE HAS A SINGLE OBJECTIVE: KILL HIM.
I DON'T GET YOU. YOU'RE ACTUALLY LAUGHING

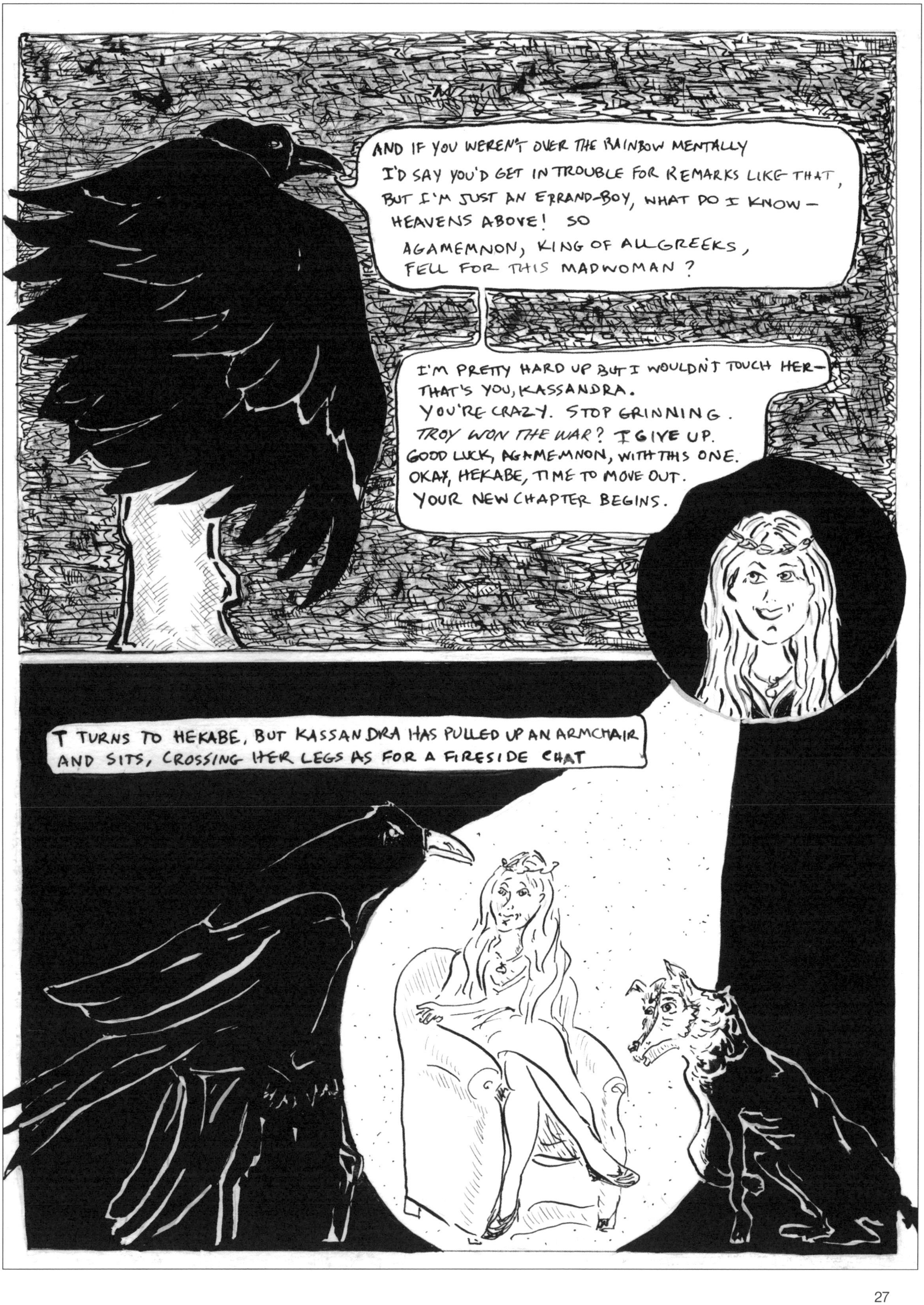
AND IF YOU WEREN'T OVER THE RAINBOW MENTALLY I'D SAY YOU'D GET IN TROUBLE FOR REMARKS LIKE THAT, BUT I'M JUST AN ERRAND-BOY, WHAT DO I KNOW – HEAVENS ABOVE! SO AGAMEMNON, KING OF ALL GREEKS, FELL FOR THIS MADWOMAN?
I'M PRETTY HARD UP BUT I WOULDN'T TOUCH HER – THAT'S YOU, KASSANDRA. YOU'RE CRAZY. STOP GRINNING. TROY WON THE WAR? I GIVE UP. GOOD LUCK, AGAMEMNON, WITH THIS ONE. OKAY, HEKABE, TIME TO MOVE OUT. YOUR NEW CHAPTER BEGINS.
T TURNS TO HEKABE, BUT KASSANDRA HAS PULLED UP AN ARMCHAIR AND SITS, CROSSING HER LEGS AS FOR A FIRESIDE CHAT

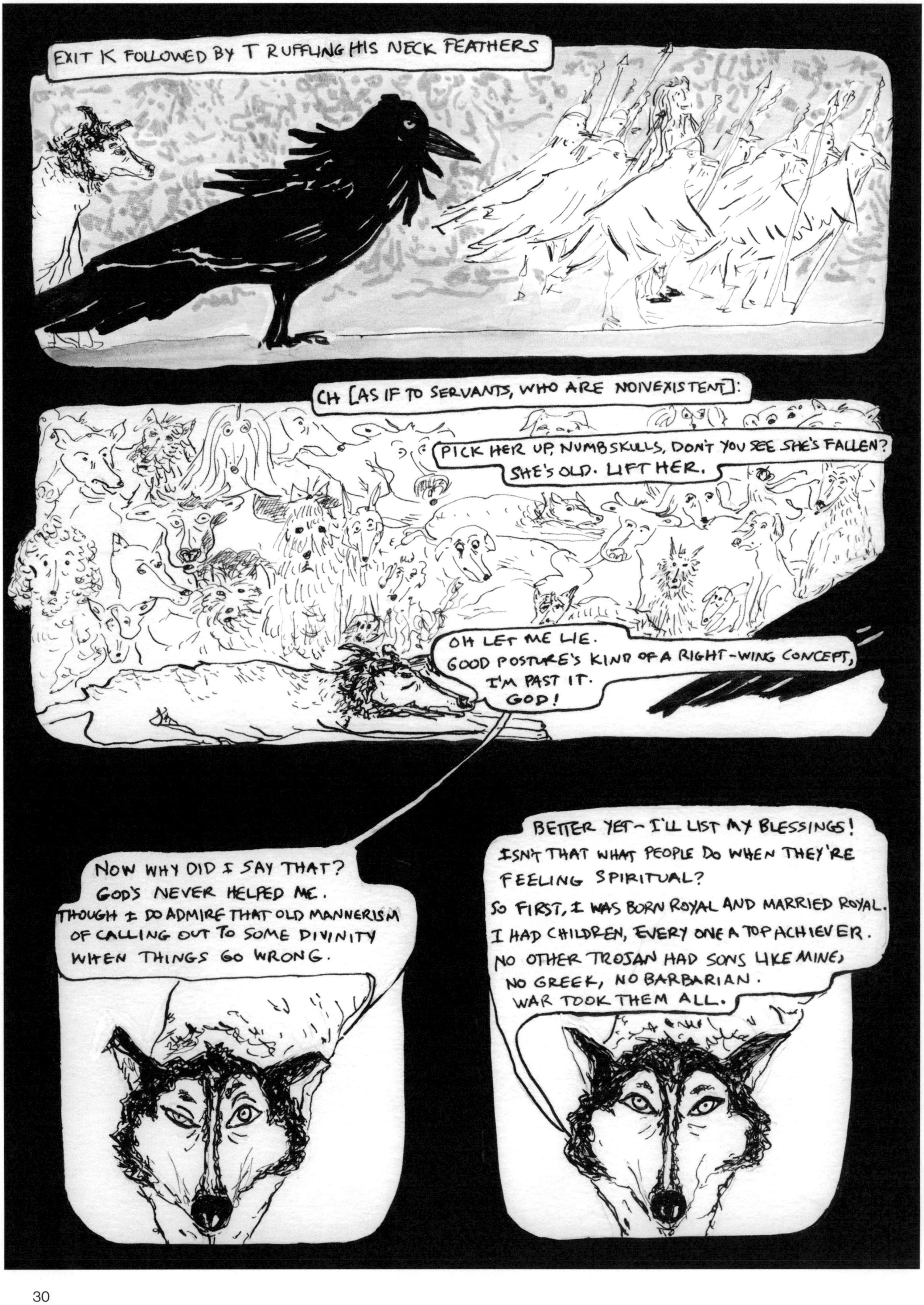

EXIT K FOLLOWED BY T RUFFLING HIS NECK FEATHERS
CH [AS IF TO SERVANTS, WHO ARE NONEXISTENT]:
PICK HER UP, NUMBSKULLS, DON'T YOU SEE SHE'S FALLEN? SHE'S OLD. LIFT HER.
OH LET ME LIE. GOOD POSTURE'S KIND OF A RIGHT-WING CONCEPT, I'M PAST IT. GOD!
NOW WHY DID I SAY THAT? GOD'S NEVER HELPED ME. THOUGH I DO ADMIRE THAT OLD MANNERISM OF CALLING OUT TO SOME DIVINITY WHEN THINGS GO WRONG.
BETTER YET - I'LL LIST MY BLESSINGS! ISN'T THAT WHAT PEOPLE DO WHEN THEY'RE FEELING SPIRITUAL? SO FIRST, I WAS BORN ROYAL AND MARRIED ROYAL. I HAD CHILDREN, EVERY ONE A TOP ACHIEVER. NO OTHER TROJAN HAD SONS LIKE MINE, NO GREEK, NO BARBARIAN. WAR TOOK THEM ALL.

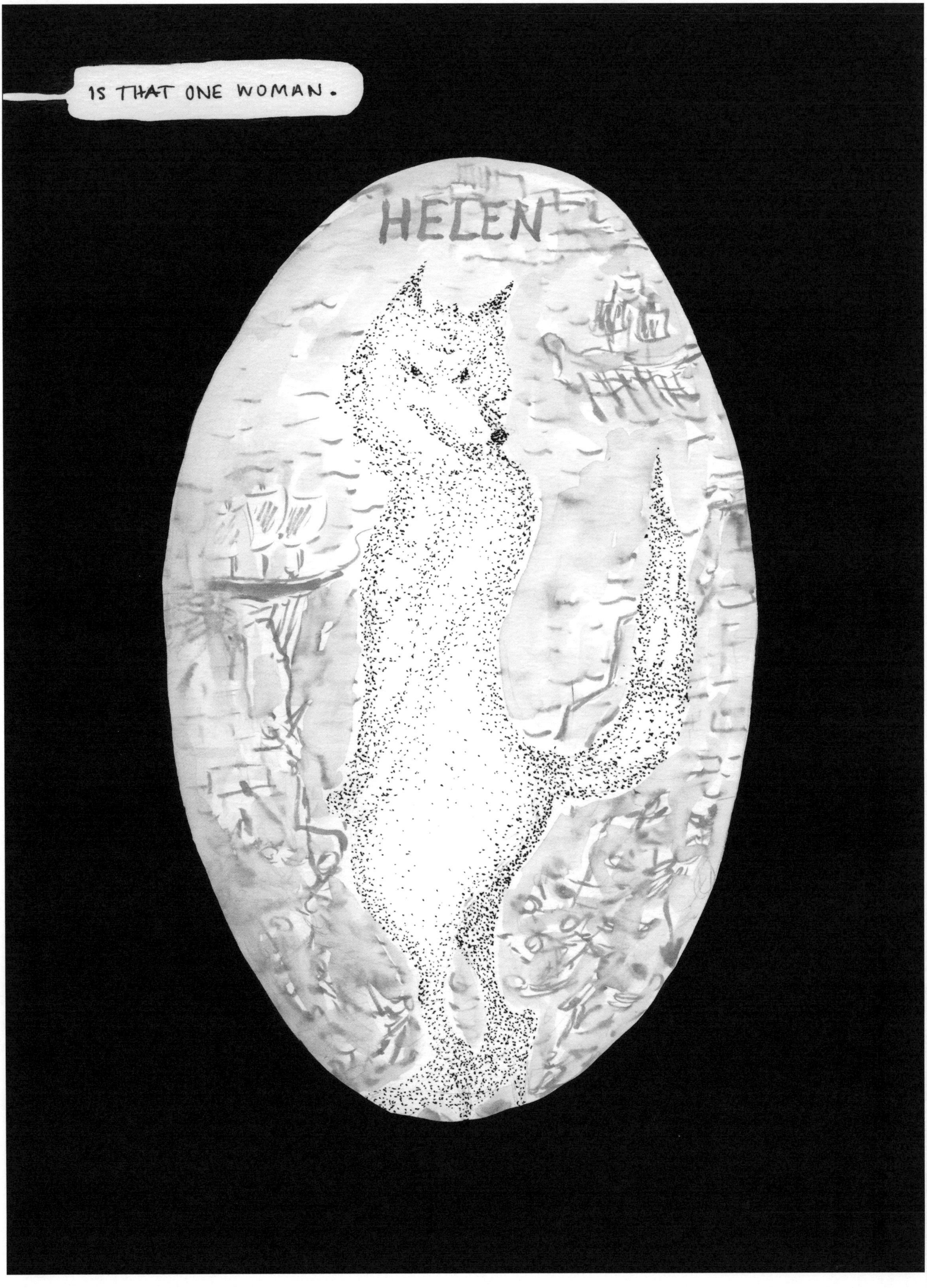
IS THAT ONE WOMAN.
HELEN

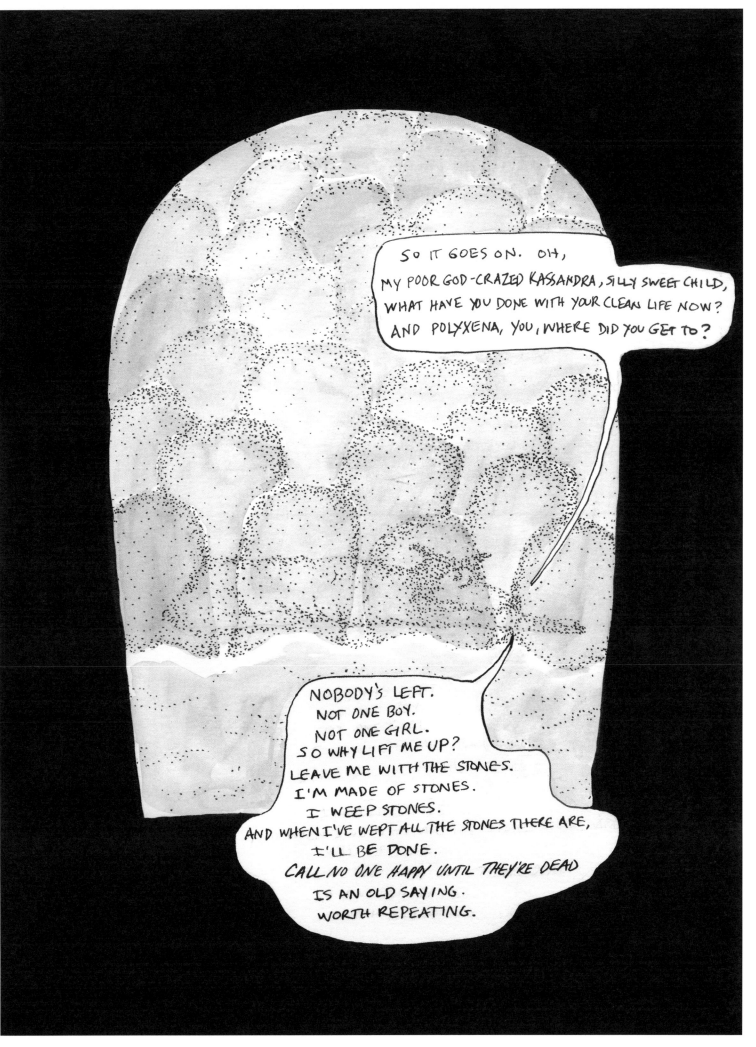

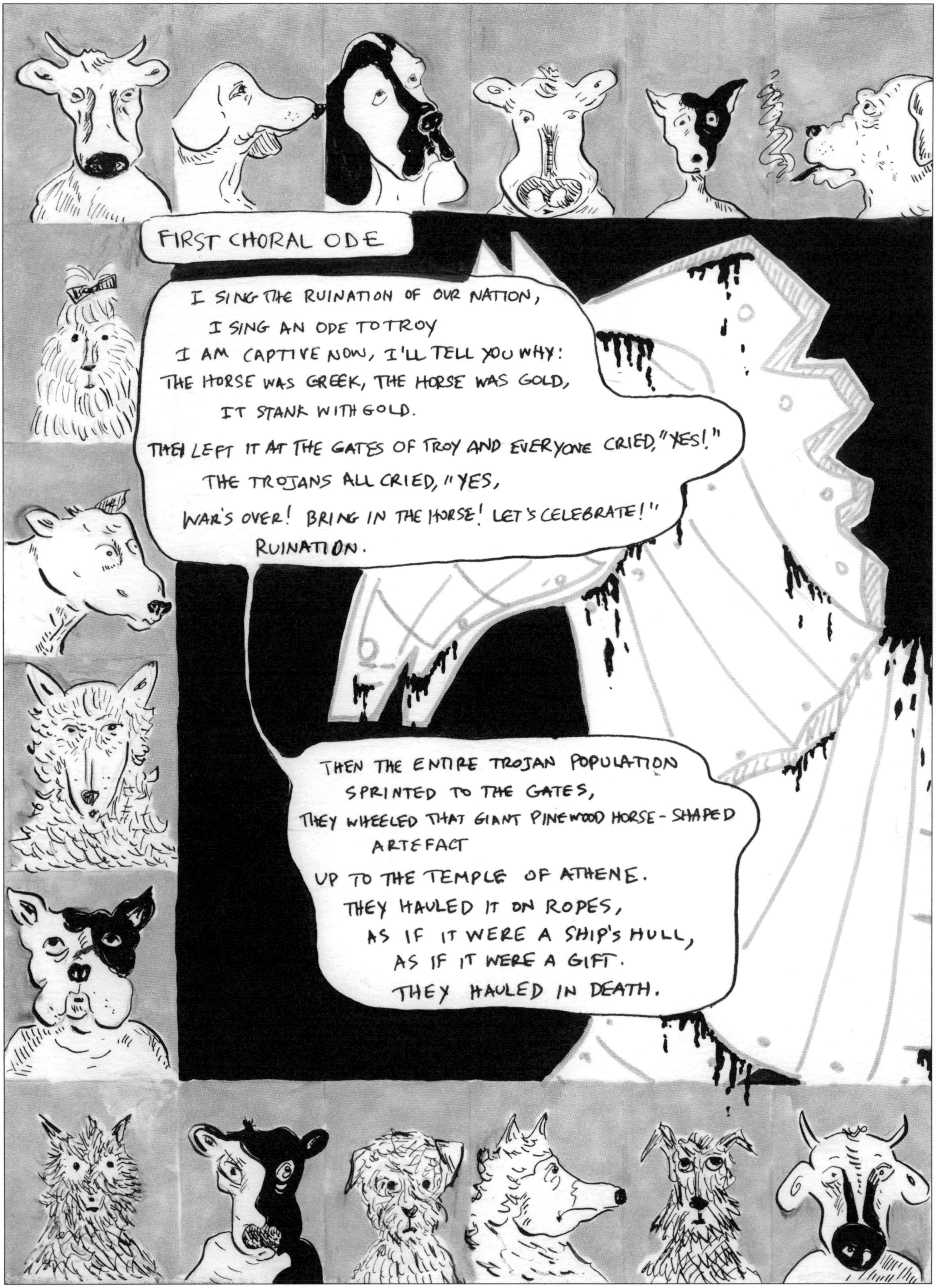
FIRST CHORAL ODE
I SING THE RUINATION OF OUR NATION, I SING AN ODE TO TROY I AM CAPTIVE NOW, I'LL TELL YOU WHY: THE HORSE WAS GREEK, THE HORSE WAS GOLD, IT STANK WITH GOLD. THEY LEFT IT AT THE GATES OF TROY AND EVERYONE CRIED, "YES!" THE TROJANS ALL CRIED, "YES, WAR'S OVER! BRING IN THE HORSE! LET'S CELEBRATE!" RUINATION.
THEN THE ENTIRE TROJAN POPULATION SPRINTED TO THE GATES, THEY WHEELED THAT GIANT PINEWOOD HORSE-SHAPED ARTEFACT UP TO THE TEMPLE OF ATHENE. THEY HAULED IT ON ROPES, AS IF IT WERE A SHIP'S HULL, AS IF IT WERE A GIFT. THEY HAULED IN DEATH.

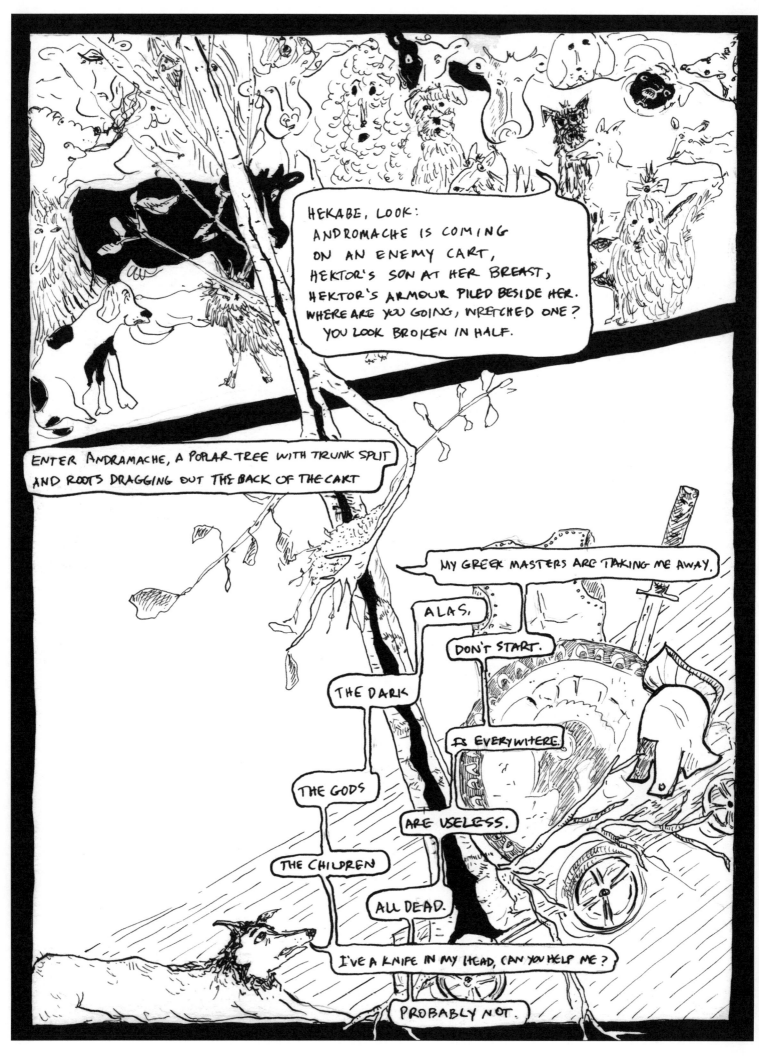

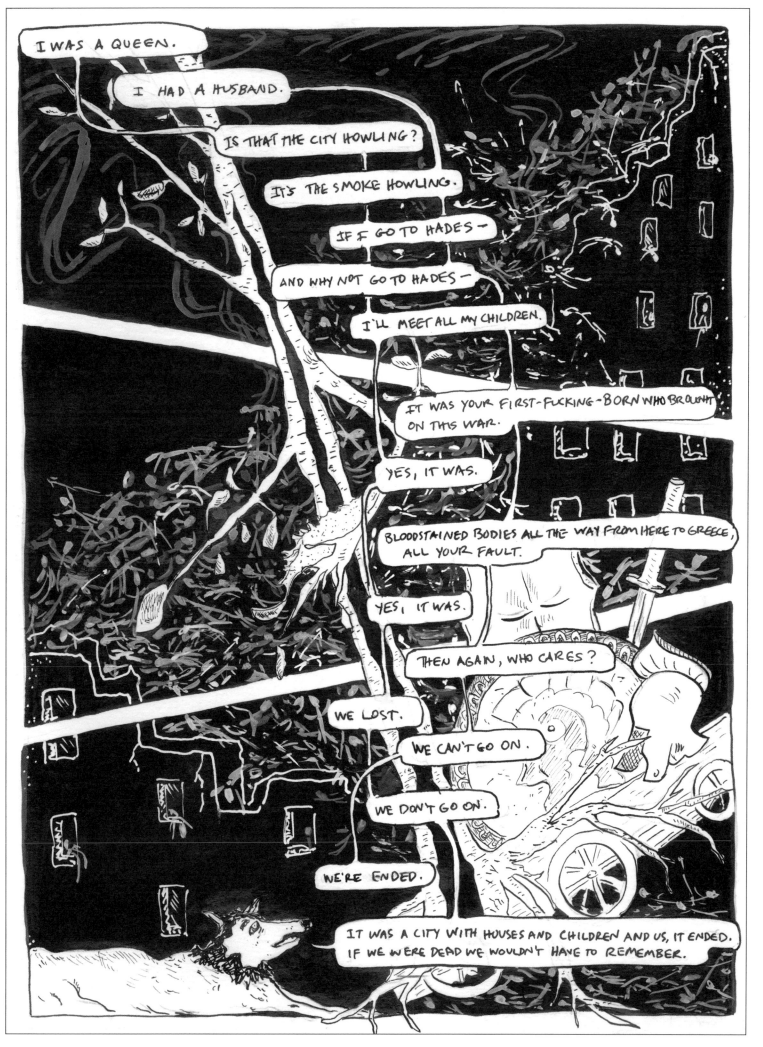

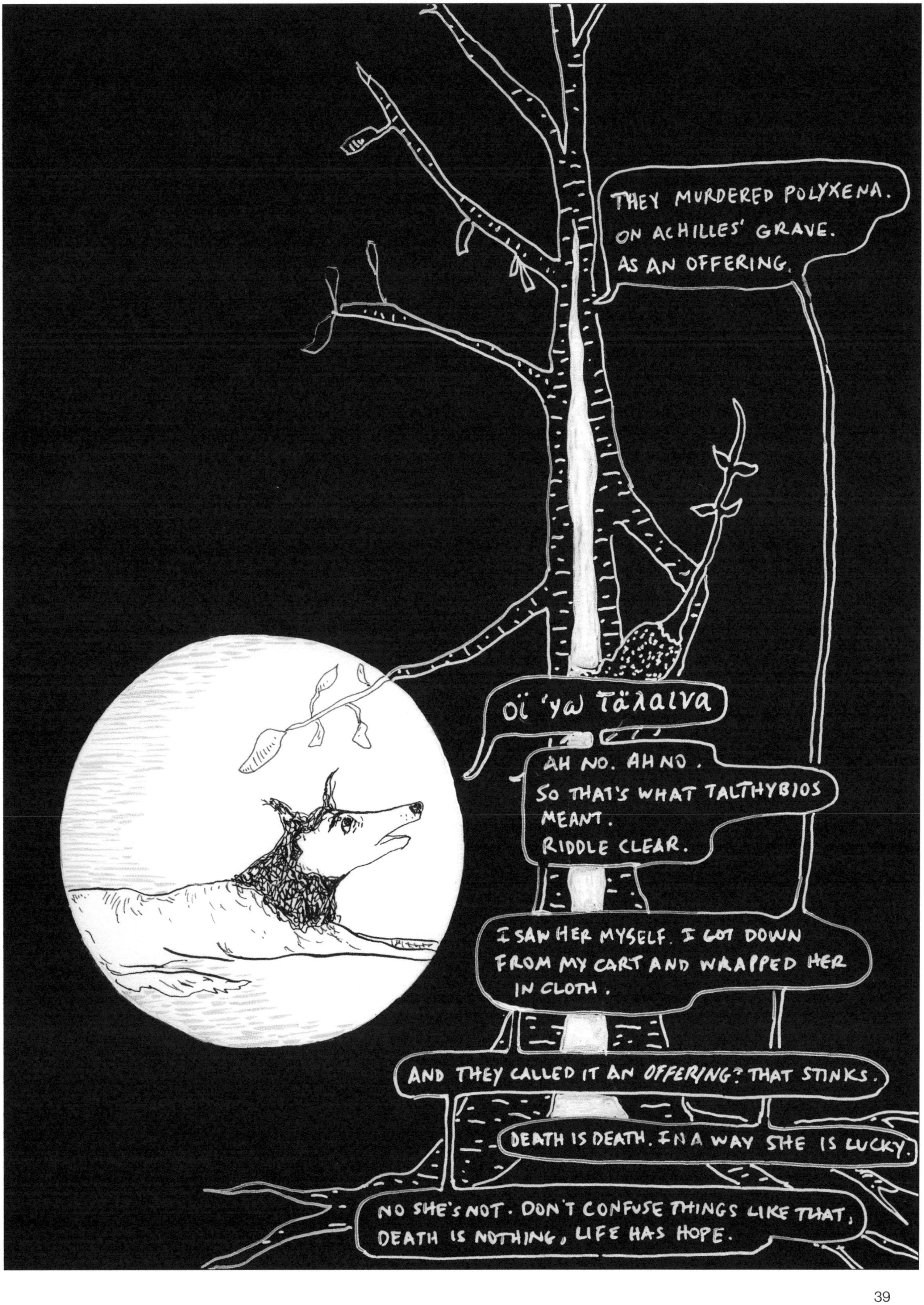
THEY MURDERED POLYXENA. ON ACHILLES' GRAVE. AS AN OFFERING.
οἴ 'γω τάλαινα
AH NO. AH NO. SO THAT'S WHAT TALTHYBIOS MEANT. RIDDLE CLEAR.
I SAW HER MYSELF. I GOT DOWN FROM MY CART AND WRAPPED HER IN CLOTH.
AND THEY CALLED IT AN *OFFERING*? THAT STINKS.
DEATH IS DEATH. IN A WAY SHE IS LUCKY.
NO SHE'S NOT. DON'T CONFUSE THINGS LIKE THAT. DEATH IS NOTHING, LIFE HAS HOPE.

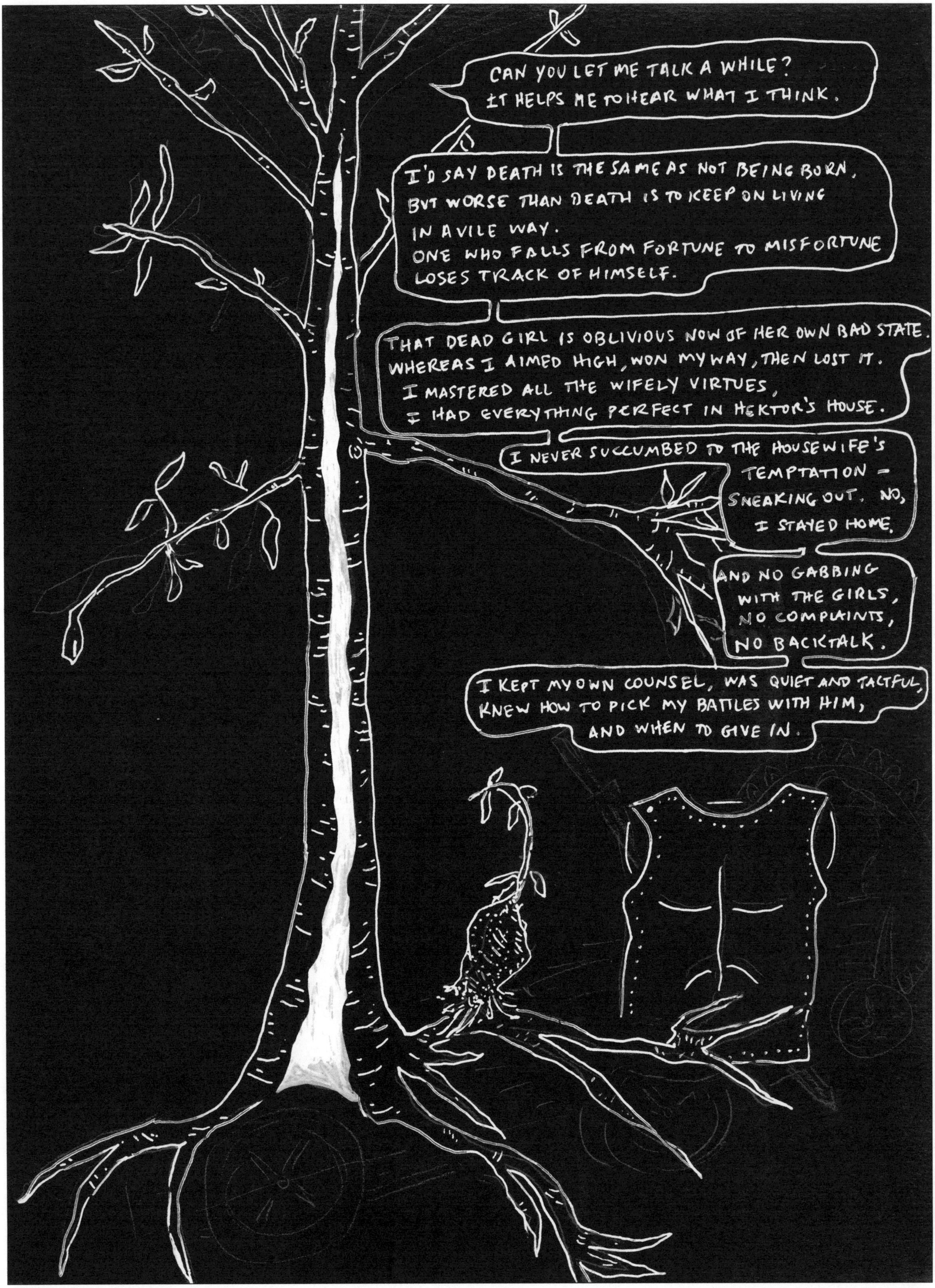
CAN YOU LET ME TALK A WHILE? IT HELPS ME TO HEAR WHAT I THINK.
I'D SAY DEATH IS THE SAME AS NOT BEING BORN, BUT WORSE THAN DEATH IS TO KEEP ON LIVING IN A VILE WAY. ONE WHO FALLS FROM FORTUNE TO MISFORTUNE LOSES TRACK OF HIMSELF.
THAT DEAD GIRL IS OBLIVIOUS NOW OF HER OWN BAD STATE. WHEREAS I AIMED HIGH, WON MY WAY, THEN LOST IT. I MASTERED ALL THE WIFELY VIRTUES, I HAD EVERYTHING PERFECT IN HEKTOR'S HOUSE.
I NEVER SUCCUMBED TO THE HOUSEWIFE'S TEMPTATION – SNEAKING OUT. NO, I STAYED HOME.
AND NO GABBING WITH THE GIRLS, NO COMPLAINTS, NO BACKTALK.
I KEPT MY OWN COUNSEL, WAS QUIET AND TACTFUL, KNEW HOW TO PICK MY BATTLES WITH HIM, AND WHEN TO GIVE IN.

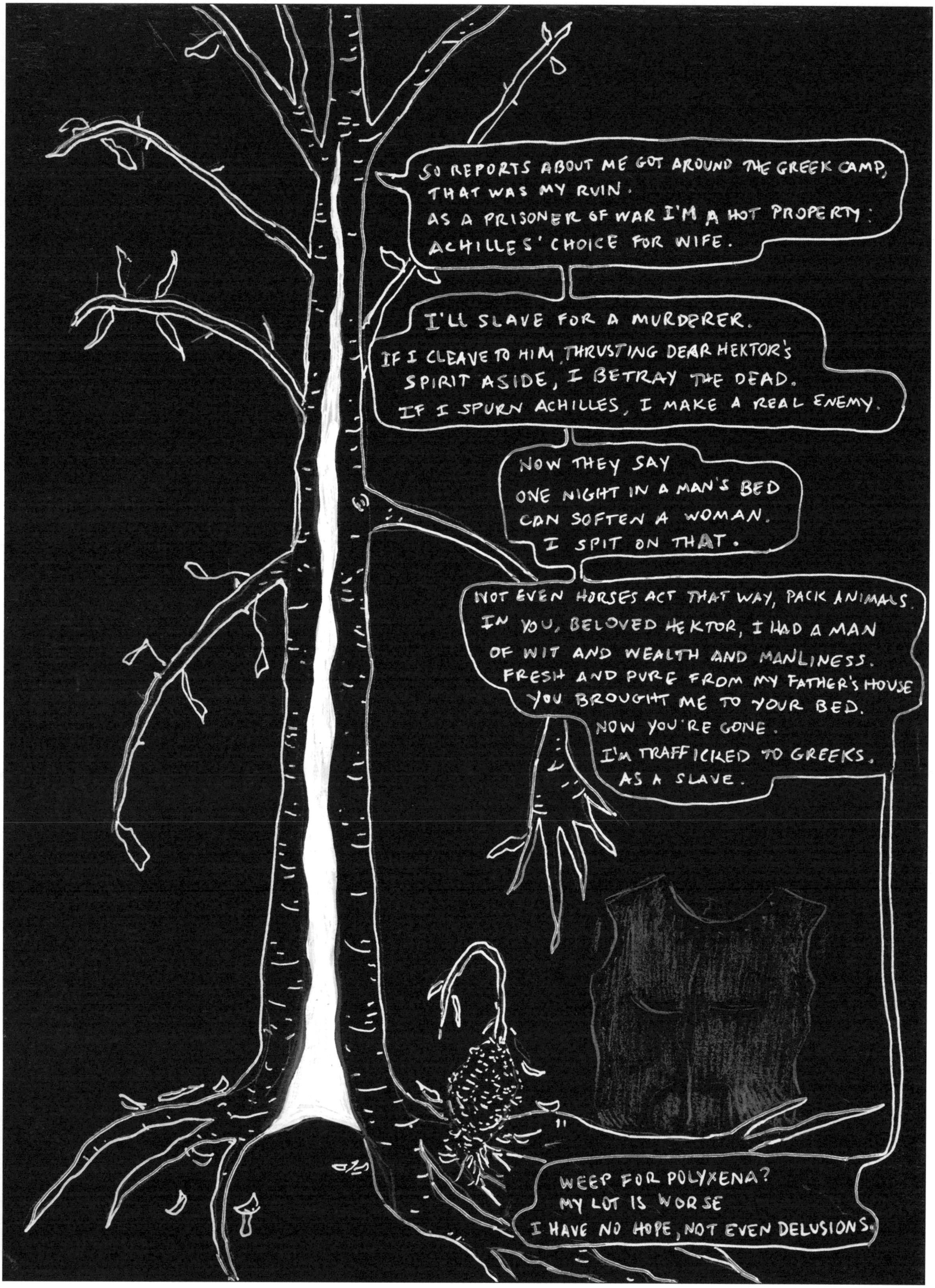
SO REPORTS ABOUT ME GOT AROUND THE GREEK CAMP, THAT WAS MY RUIN. AS A PRISONER OF WAR I'M A HOT PROPERTY: ACHILLES' CHOICE FOR WIFE.
I'LL SLAVE FOR A MURDERER. IF I CLEAVE TO HIM, THRUSTING DEAR HEKTOR'S SPIRIT ASIDE, I BETRAY THE DEAD. IF I SPURN ACHILLES, I MAKE A REAL ENEMY.
NOW THEY SAY ONE NIGHT IN A MAN'S BED CAN SOFTEN A WOMAN. I SPIT ON THAT.
NOT EVEN HORSES ACT THAT WAY, PACK ANIMALS. IN YOU, BELOVED HEKTOR, I HAD A MAN OF WIT AND WEALTH AND MANLINESS. FRESH AND PURE FROM MY FATHER'S HOUSE YOU BROUGHT ME TO YOUR BED. NOW YOU'RE GONE. I'M TRAFFICKED TO GREEKS. AS A SLAVE.
WEEP FOR POLYXENA? MY LOT IS WORSE I HAVE NO HOPE, NOT EVEN DELUSIONS.

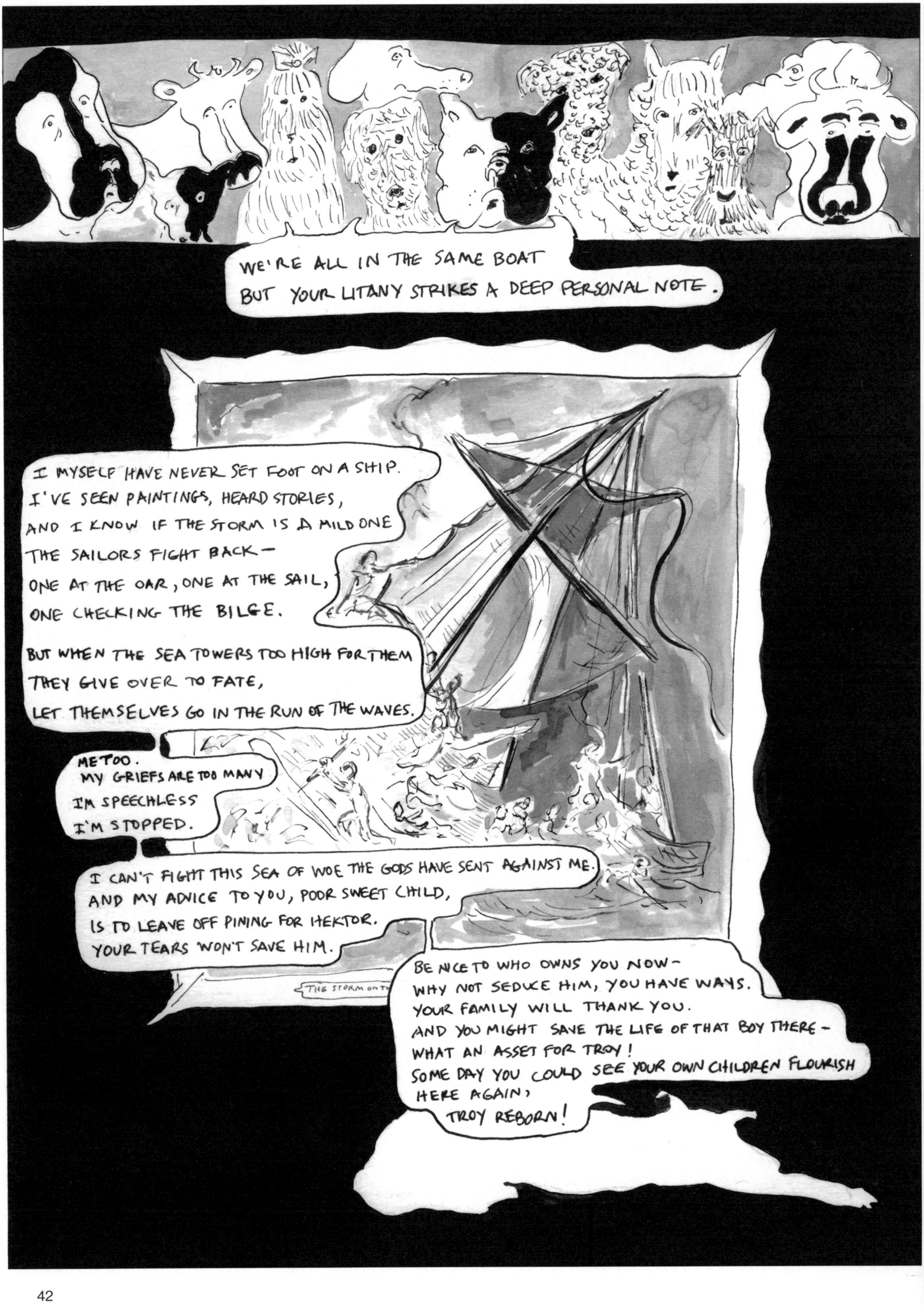
WE'RE ALL IN THE SAME BOAT
BUT YOUR LITANY STRIKES A DEEP PERSONAL NOTE.
I MYSELF HAVE NEVER SET FOOT ON A SHIP. I'VE SEEN PAINTINGS, HEARD STORIES, AND I KNOW IF THE STORM IS A MILD ONE THE SAILORS FIGHT BACK — ONE AT THE OAR, ONE AT THE SAIL, ONE CHECKING THE BILGE.
BUT WHEN THE SEA TOWERS TOO HIGH FOR THEM THEY GIVE OVER TO FATE, LET THEMSELVES GO IN THE RUN OF THE WAVES.
ME TOO. MY GRIEFS ARE TOO MANY I'M SPEECHLESS I'M STOPPED.
I CAN'T FIGHT THIS SEA OF WOE THE GODS HAVE SENT AGAINST ME. AND MY ADVICE TO YOU, POOR SWEET CHILD, IS TO LEAVE OFF PINING FOR HEKTOR. YOUR TEARS WON'T SAVE HIM.
BE NICE TO WHO OWNS YOU NOW — WHY NOT SEDUCE HIM, YOU HAVE WAYS. YOUR FAMILY WILL THANK YOU. AND YOU MIGHT SAVE THE LIFE OF THAT BOY THERE — WHAT AN ASSET FOR TROY! SOME DAY YOU COULD SEE YOUR OWN CHILDREN FLOURISH HERE AGAIN, TROY REBORN!

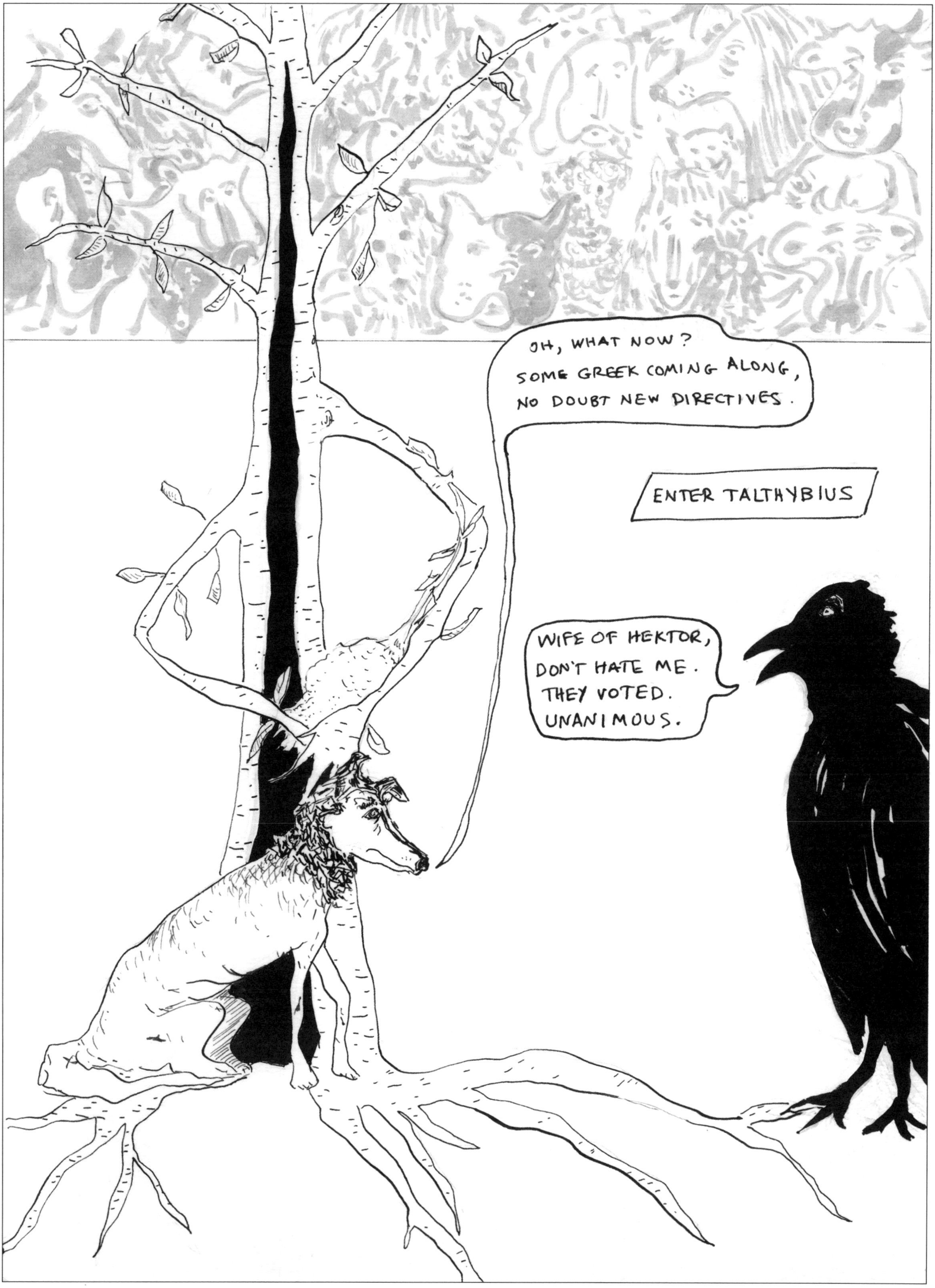
OH, WHAT NOW?
SOME GREEK COMING ALONG,
NO DOUBT NEW DIRECTIVES.
ENTER TALTHYBIUS
WIFE OF HEKTOR,
DON'T HATE ME.
THEY VOTED.
UNANIMOUS.

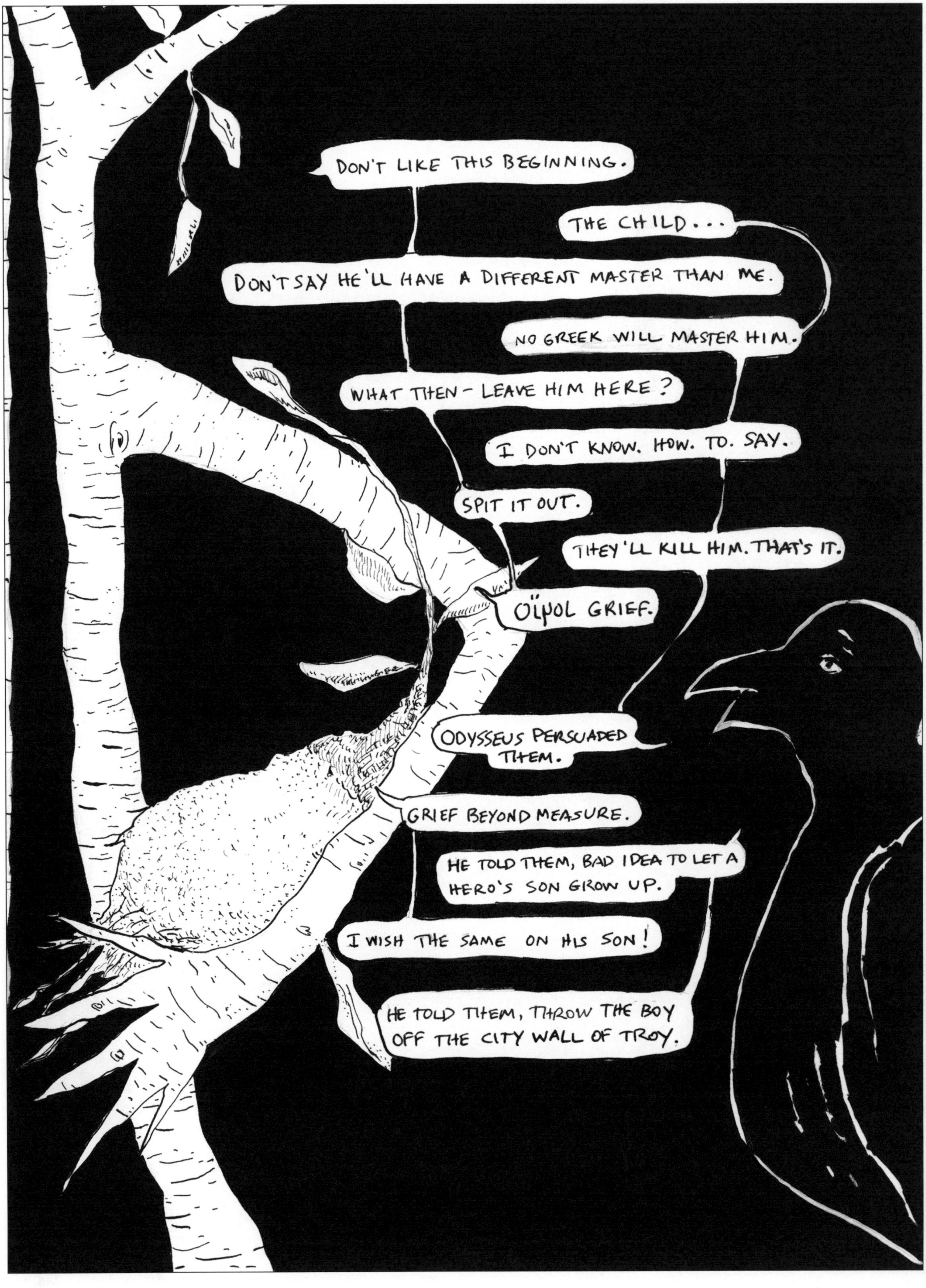
DON'T LIKE THIS BEGINNING.
THE CHILD...
DON'T SAY HE'LL HAVE A DIFFERENT MASTER THAN ME.
NO GREEK WILL MASTER HIM.
WHAT THEN - LEAVE HIM HERE?
I DON'T KNOW. HOW. TO. SAY.
SPIT IT OUT.
THEY'LL KILL HIM. THAT'S IT.
Oϊμοι GRIEF.
ODYSSEUS PERSUADED THEM.
GRIEF BEYOND MEASURE.
HE TOLD THEM, BAD IDEA TO LET A HERO'S SON GROW UP.
I WISH THE SAME ON HIS SON!
HE TOLD THEM, THROW THE BOY OFF THE CITY WALL OF TROY.

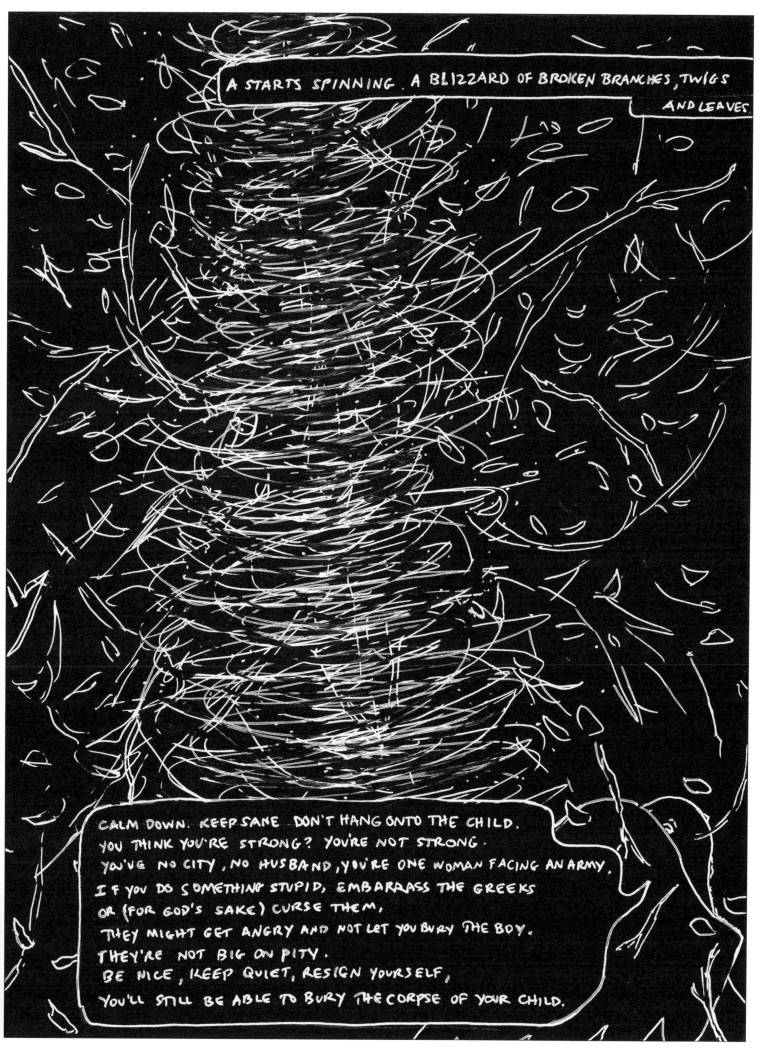

A STARTS SPINNING. A BLIZZARD OF BROKEN BRANCHES, TWIGS AND LEAVES

CALM DOWN. KEEP SANE. DON'T HANG ONTO THE CHILD.
YOU THINK YOU'RE STRONG? YOU'RE NOT STRONG.
YOU'VE NO CITY, NO HUSBAND, YOU'RE ONE WOMAN FACING AN ARMY.
IF YOU DO SOMETHING STUPID, EMBARRASS THE GREEKS
OR (FOR GOD'S SAKE) CURSE THEM,
THEY MIGHT GET ANGRY AND NOT LET YOU BURY THE BOY.
THEY'RE NOT BIG ON PITY.
BE NICE, KEEP QUIET, RESIGN YOURSELF,
YOU'LL STILL BE ABLE TO BURY THE CORPSE OF YOUR CHILD.

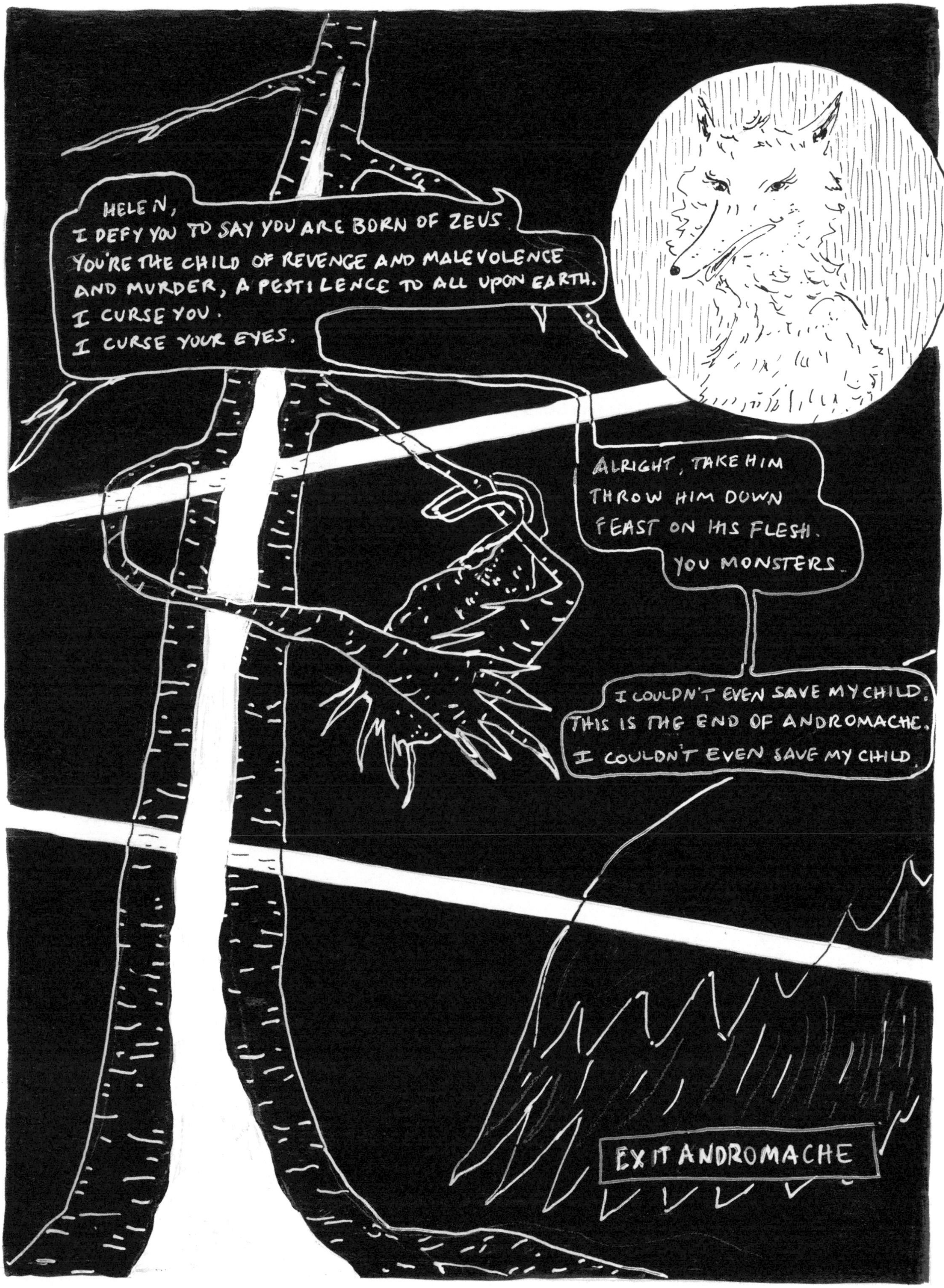
HELEN,
I DEFY YOU TO SAY YOU ARE BORN OF ZEUS.
YOU'RE THE CHILD OF REVENGE AND MALEVOLENCE
AND MURDER, A PESTILENCE TO ALL UPON EARTH.
I CURSE YOU.
I CURSE YOUR EYES.
ALRIGHT, TAKE HIM
THROW HIM DOWN
FEAST ON HIS FLESH.
YOU MONSTERS.
I COULDN'T EVEN SAVE MY CHILD.
THIS IS THE END OF ANDROMACHE.
I COULDN'T EVEN SAVE MY CHILD.
EXIT ANDROMACHE

48

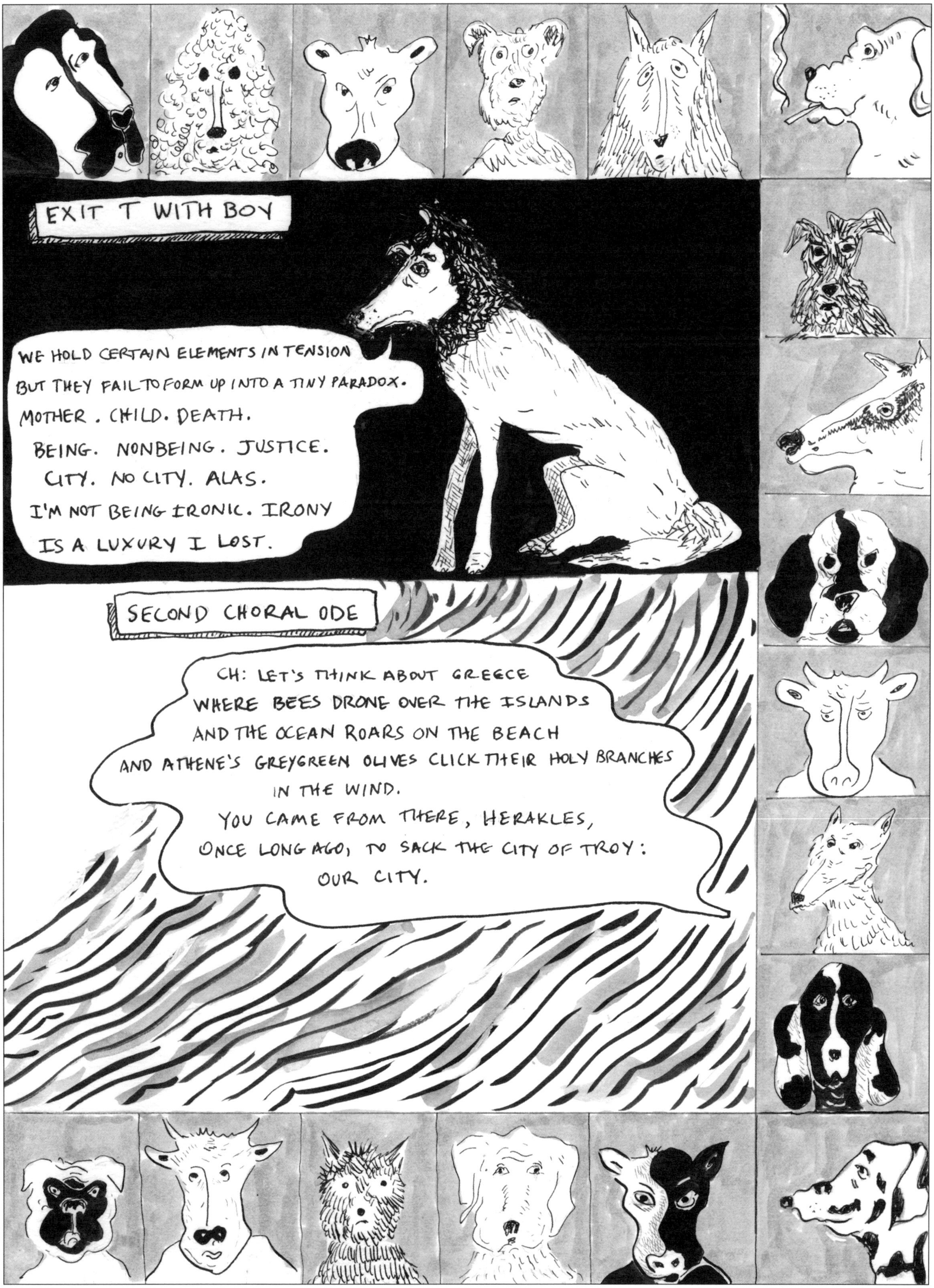
EXIT T WITH BOY
WE HOLD CERTAIN ELEMENTS IN TENSION BUT THEY FAIL TO FORM UP INTO A TINY PARADOX. MOTHER. CHILD. DEATH. BEING. NONBEING. JUSTICE. CITY. NO CITY. ALAS. I'M NOT BEING IRONIC. IRONY IS A LUXURY I LOST.
SECOND CHORAL ODE
CH: LET'S THINK ABOUT GREECE WHERE BEES DRONE OVER THE ISLANDS AND THE OCEAN ROARS ON THE BEACH AND ATHENE'S GREYGREEN OLIVES CLICK THEIR HOLY BRANCHES IN THE WIND. YOU CAME FROM THERE, HERAKLES, ONCE LONG AGO, TO SACK THE CITY OF TROY: OUR CITY.

CH: YOU BROUGHT SHIPS AND HORSES AND MURDER,
YOU BROUGHT THE UNERRING AIM OF YOUR BOW.
TROY WAS A MASTERPIECE OF WALLS AND TOWERS,
MEASURED BY PLUMB LINE AND CHISELED OF STONE.
YOU BEAT IT TO THE GROUND.
YOUR SPEARS AND SWORDS AND ARROWS
RAINED BLOOD ON TROY.
IT'S NOT AS IF WE HAVE NO FRIENDS AMONG THE GODS.
DEAR GANYMEDE, YOU WHO WERE TAKEN UP
TO BE BUTT-BOY OF ZEUS: HOW ELEGANTLY
YOU FLOAT THERE, FILLING
GOLDEN CUPS WITH WINE,
WHILE DOWN HERE
THE CITY IS IN CONFLAGRATION AND THE VERY BEACHES
TROY
ROAR LIKE WOMEN'S VOICES,
FOR THEIR HUSBANDS, THEIR CHILDREN,
THEIR MOTHERS LOST.

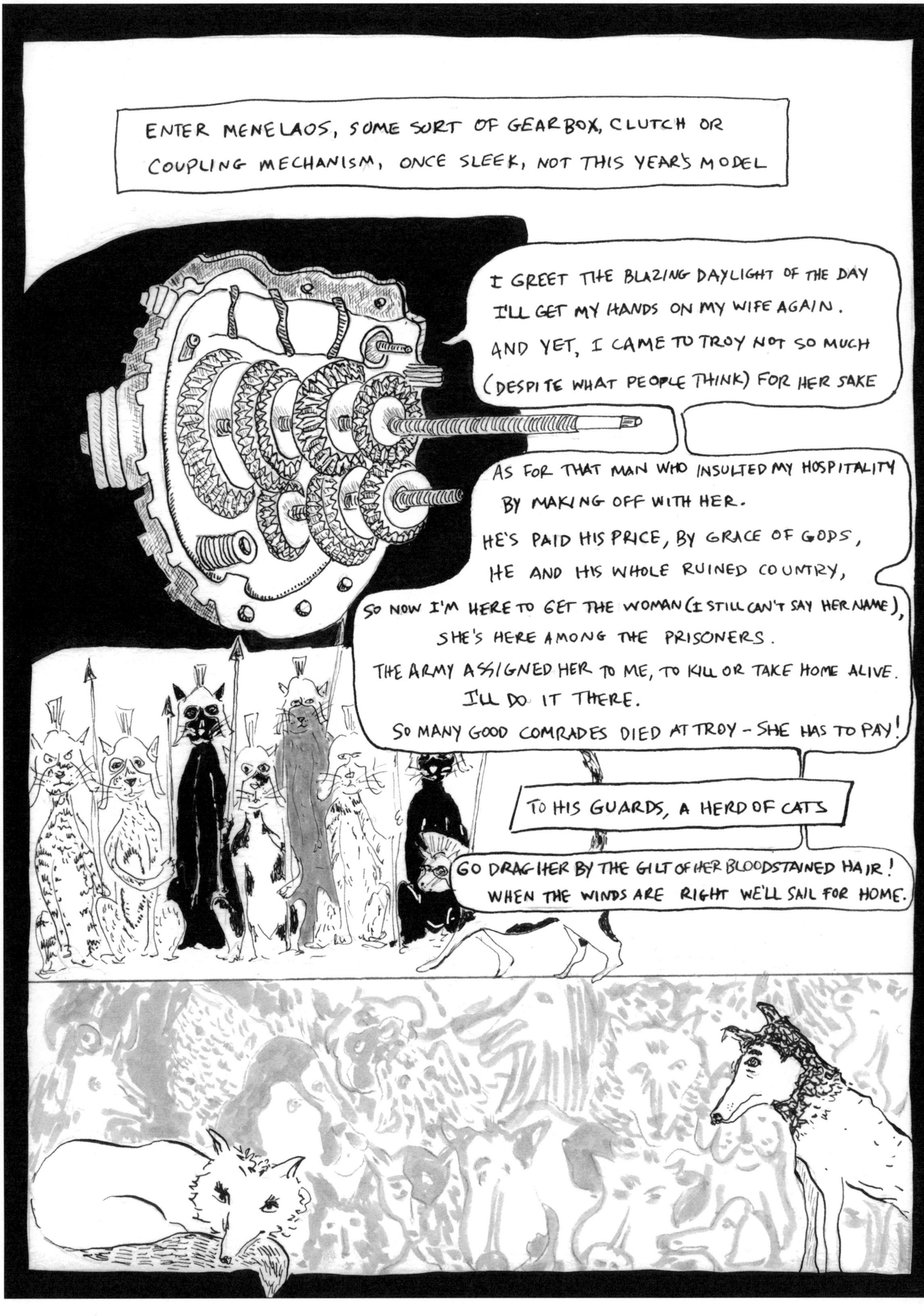
ENTER MENELAOS, SOME SORT OF GEARBOX, CLUTCH OR COUPLING MECHANISM, ONCE SLEEK, NOT THIS YEAR'S MODEL
I GREET THE BLAZING DAYLIGHT OF THE DAY I'LL GET MY HANDS ON MY WIFE AGAIN. AND YET, I CAME TO TROY NOT SO MUCH (DESPITE WHAT PEOPLE THINK) FOR HER SAKE
AS FOR THAT MAN WHO INSULTED MY HOSPITALITY BY MAKING OFF WITH HER. HE'S PAID HIS PRICE, BY GRACE OF GODS, HE AND HIS WHOLE RUINED COUNTRY, SO NOW I'M HERE TO GET THE WOMAN (I STILL CAN'T SAY HER NAME), SHE'S HERE AMONG THE PRISONERS. THE ARMY ASSIGNED HER TO ME, TO KILL OR TAKE HOME ALIVE. I'LL DO IT THERE. SO MANY GOOD COMRADES DIED AT TROY - SHE HAS TO PAY!
TO HIS GUARDS, A HERD OF CATS
GO DRAG HER BY THE GILT OF HER BLOODSTAINED HAIR! WHEN THE WINDS ARE RIGHT WE'LL SAIL FOR HOME.

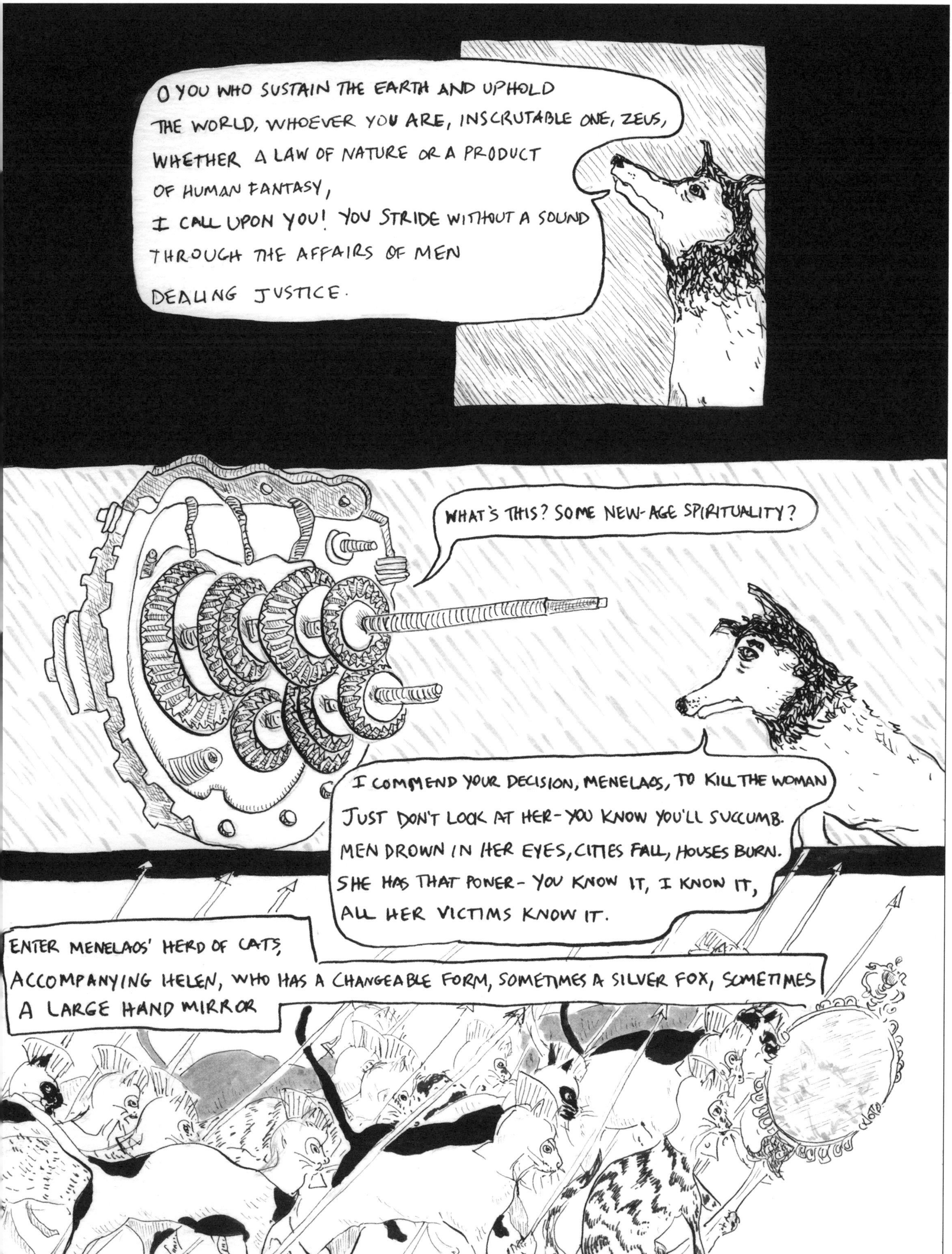
O YOU WHO SUSTAIN THE EARTH AND UPHOLD THE WORLD, WHOEVER YOU ARE, INSCRUTABLE ONE, ZEUS, WHETHER A LAW OF NATURE OR A PRODUCT OF HUMAN FANTASY, I CALL UPON YOU! YOU STRIDE WITHOUT A SOUND THROUGH THE AFFAIRS OF MEN DEALING JUSTICE.
WHAT'S THIS? SOME NEW-AGE SPIRITUALITY?
I COMMEND YOUR DECISION, MENELAOS, TO KILL THE WOMAN JUST DON'T LOOK AT HER - YOU KNOW YOU'LL SUCCUMB. MEN DROWN IN HER EYES, CITIES FALL, HOUSES BURN. SHE HAS THAT POWER - YOU KNOW IT, I KNOW IT, ALL HER VICTIMS KNOW IT.
ENTER MENELAOS' HERD OF CATS, ACCOMPANYING HELEN, WHO HAS A CHANGEABLE FORM, SOMETIMES A SILVER FOX, SOMETIMES A LARGE HAND MIRROR

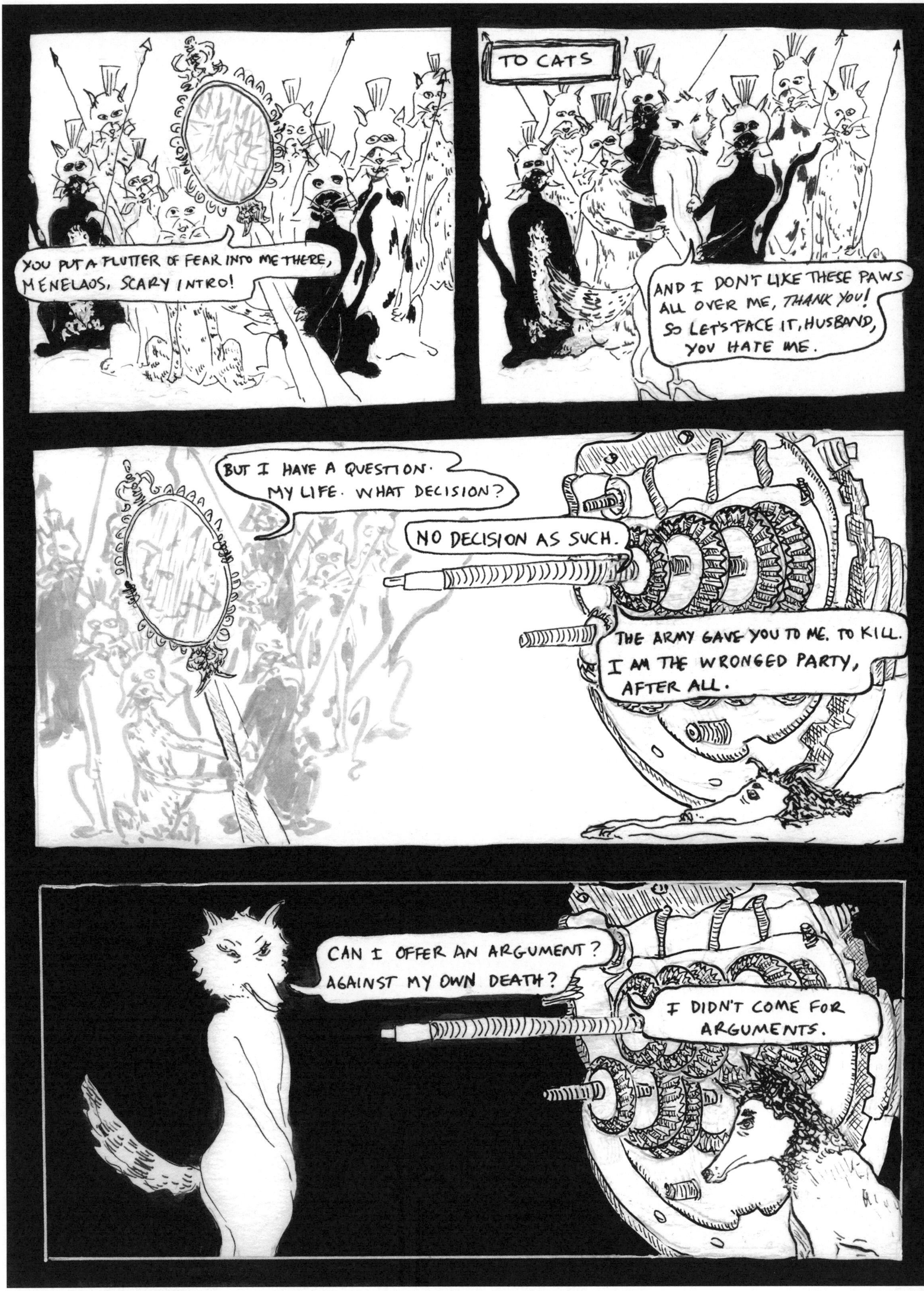
YOU PUT A FLUTTER OF FEAR INTO ME THERE, MENELAOS, SCARY INTRO!
TO CATS
AND I DON'T LIKE THESE PAWS ALL OVER ME, THANK YOU! SO LET'S FACE IT, HUSBAND, YOU HATE ME.
BUT I HAVE A QUESTION. MY LIFE. WHAT DECISION?
NO DECISION AS SUCH.
THE ARMY GAVE YOU TO ME. TO KILL. I AM THE WRONGED PARTY, AFTER ALL.
CAN I OFFER AN ARGUMENT? AGAINST MY OWN DEATH?
I DIDN'T COME FOR ARGUMENTS.

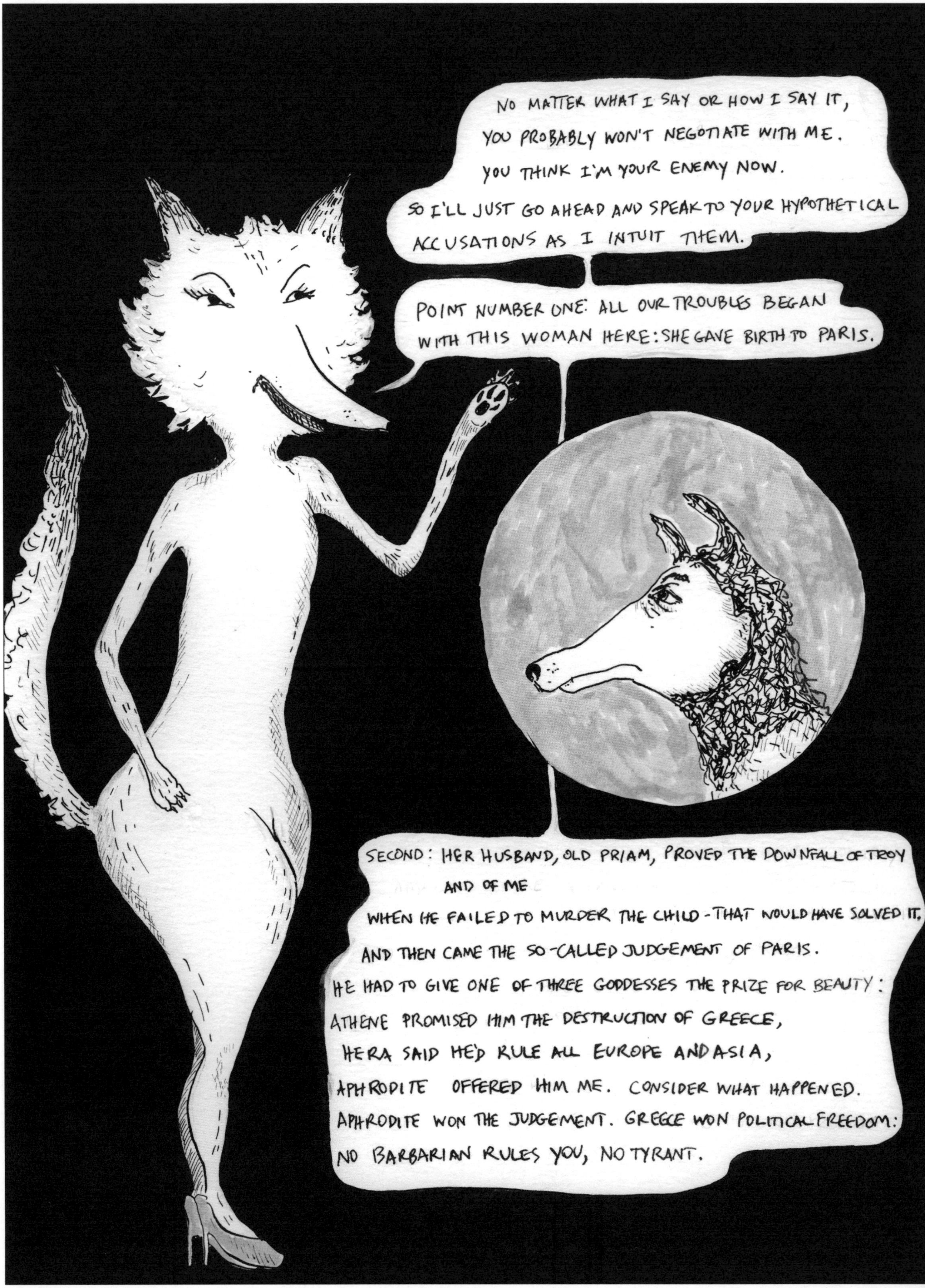
NO MATTER WHAT I SAY OR HOW I SAY IT, YOU PROBABLY WON'T NEGOTIATE WITH ME. YOU THINK I'M YOUR ENEMY NOW. SO I'LL JUST GO AHEAD AND SPEAK TO YOUR HYPOTHETICAL ACCUSATIONS AS I INTUIT THEM.
POINT NUMBER ONE: ALL OUR TROUBLES BEGAN WITH THIS WOMAN HERE: SHE GAVE BIRTH TO PARIS.
SECOND: HER HUSBAND, OLD PRIAM, PROVED THE DOWNFALL OF TROY AND OF ME WHEN HE FAILED TO MURDER THE CHILD - THAT WOULD HAVE SOLVED IT. AND THEN CAME THE SO-CALLED JUDGEMENT OF PARIS. HE HAD TO GIVE ONE OF THREE GODDESSES THE PRIZE FOR BEAUTY: ATHENE PROMISED HIM THE DESTRUCTION OF GREECE, HERA SAID HE'D RULE ALL EUROPE AND ASIA, APHRODITE OFFERED HIM ME. CONSIDER WHAT HAPPENED. APHRODITE WON THE JUDGEMENT. GREECE WON POLITICAL FREEDOM: NO BARBARIAN RULES YOU, NO TYRANT.

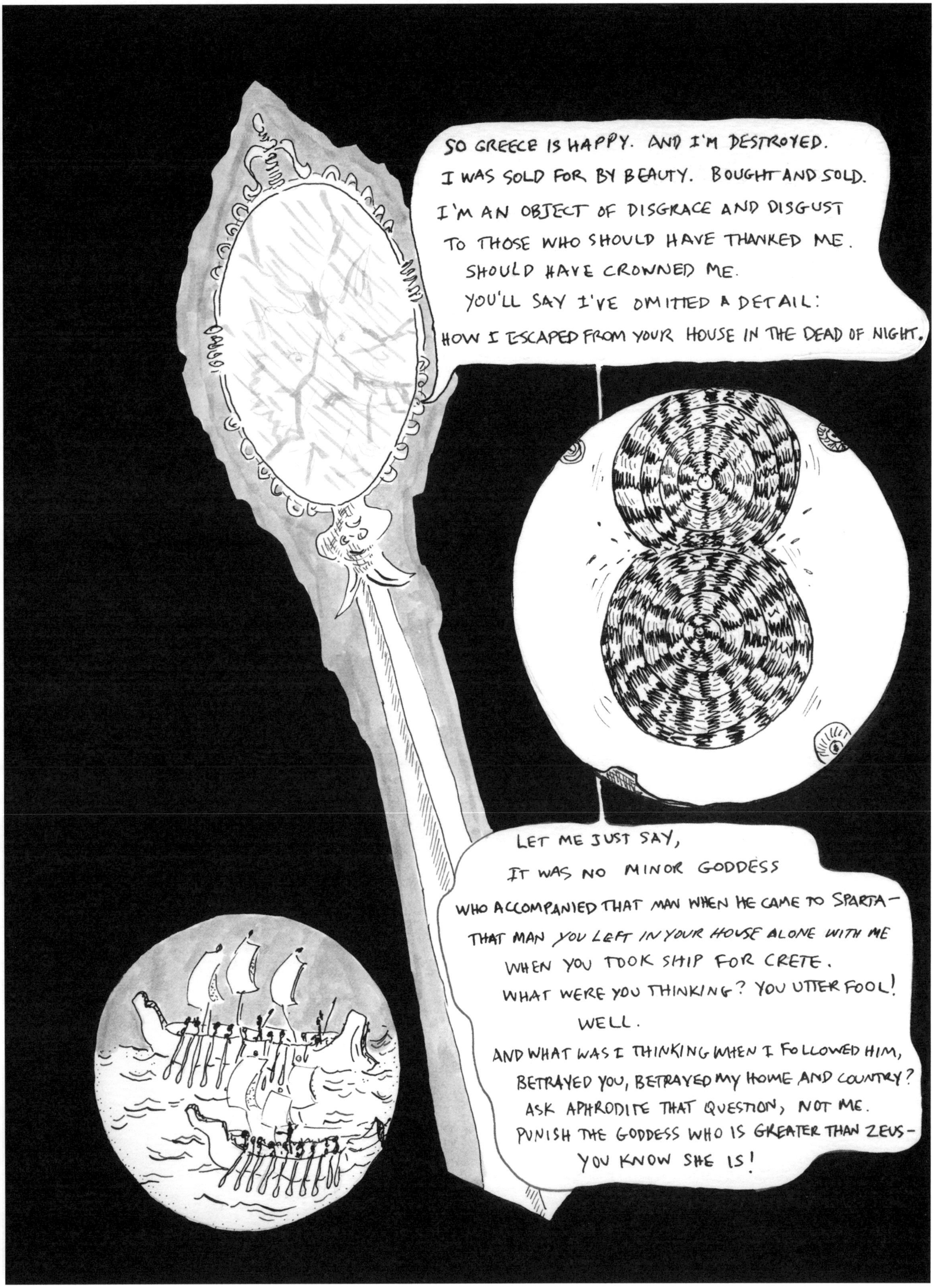
SO GREECE IS HAPPY. AND I'M DESTROYED.
I WAS SOLD FOR BY BEAUTY. BOUGHT AND SOLD.
I'M AN OBJECT OF DISGRACE AND DISGUST
TO THOSE WHO SHOULD HAVE THANKED ME.
SHOULD HAVE CROWNED ME.
YOU'LL SAY I'VE OMITTED A DETAIL:
HOW I ESCAPED FROM YOUR HOUSE IN THE DEAD OF NIGHT.
LET ME JUST SAY,
IT WAS NO MINOR GODDESS
WHO ACCOMPANIED THAT MAN WHEN HE CAME TO SPARTA—
THAT MAN *YOU LEFT IN YOUR HOUSE ALONE WITH ME*
WHEN YOU TOOK SHIP FOR CRETE.
WHAT WERE YOU THINKING? YOU UTTER FOOL!
WELL.
AND WHAT WAS I THINKING WHEN I FOLLOWED HIM,
BETRAYED YOU, BETRAYED MY HOME AND COUNTRY?
ASK APHRODITE THAT QUESTION, NOT ME.
PUNISH THE GODDESS WHO IS GREATER THAN ZEUS—
YOU KNOW SHE IS!

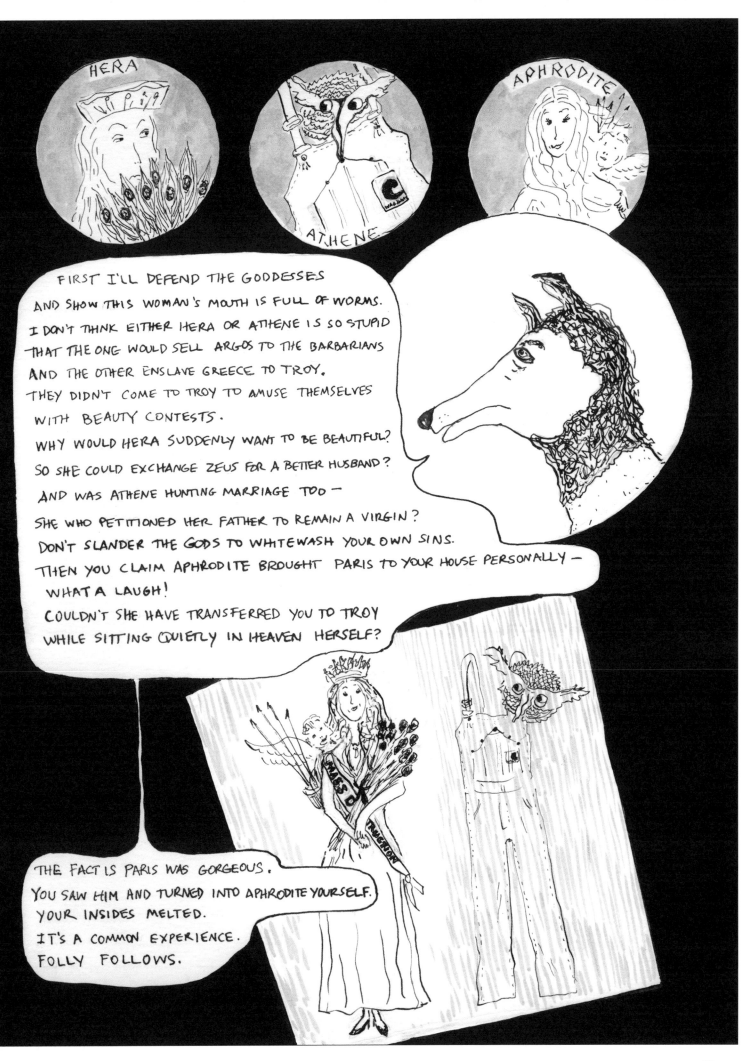

FIRST I'LL DEFEND THE GODDESSES
AND SHOW THIS WOMAN'S MOUTH IS FULL OF WORMS.
I DON'T THINK EITHER HERA OR ATHENE IS SO STUPID
THAT THE ONE WOULD SELL ARGOS TO THE BARBARIANS
AND THE OTHER ENSLAVE GREECE TO TROY.
THEY DIDN'T COME TO TROY TO AMUSE THEMSELVES
WITH BEAUTY CONTESTS.
WHY WOULD HERA SUDDENLY WANT TO BE BEAUTIFUL?
SO SHE COULD EXCHANGE ZEUS FOR A BETTER HUSBAND?
AND WAS ATHENE HUNTING MARRIAGE TOO —
SHE WHO PETITIONED HER FATHER TO REMAIN A VIRGIN?
DON'T SLANDER THE GODS TO WHITEWASH YOUR OWN SINS.
THEN YOU CLAIM APHRODITE BROUGHT PARIS TO YOUR HOUSE PERSONALLY —
WHAT A LAUGH!
COULDN'T SHE HAVE TRANSFERRED YOU TO TROY
WHILE SITTING QUIETLY IN HEAVEN HERSELF?

THE FACT IS PARIS WAS GORGEOUS.
YOU SAW HIM AND TURNED INTO APHRODITE YOURSELF.
YOUR INSIDES MELTED.
IT'S A COMMON EXPERIENCE.
FOLLY FOLLOWS.

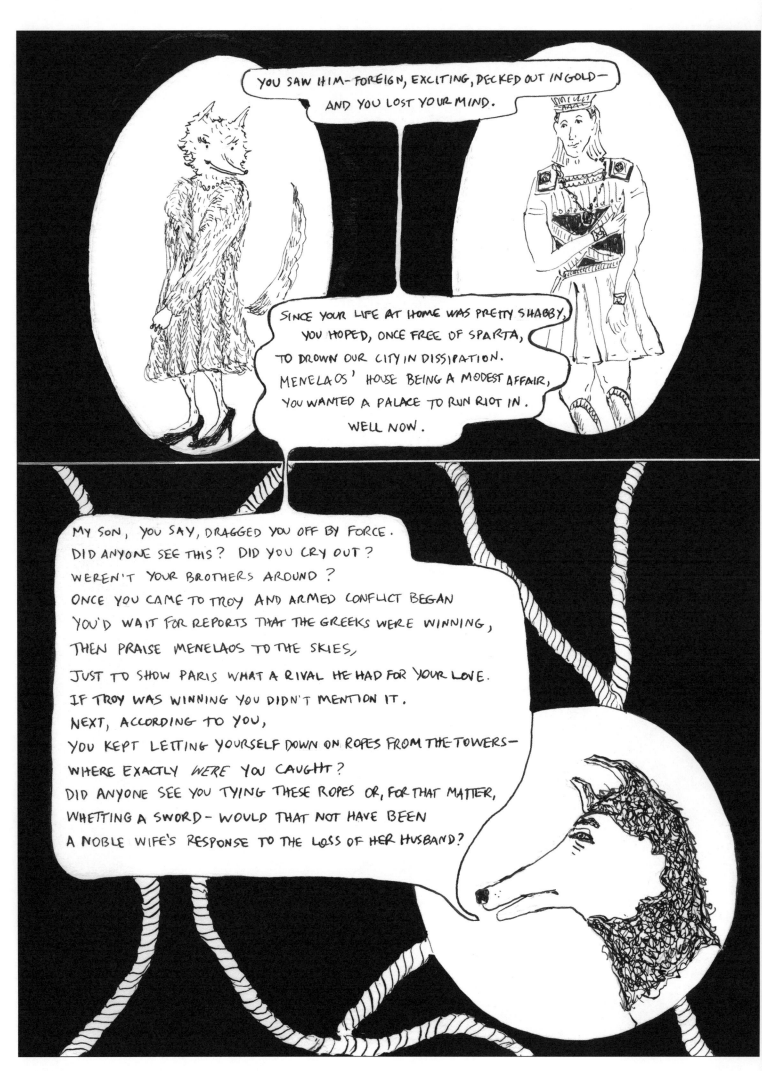

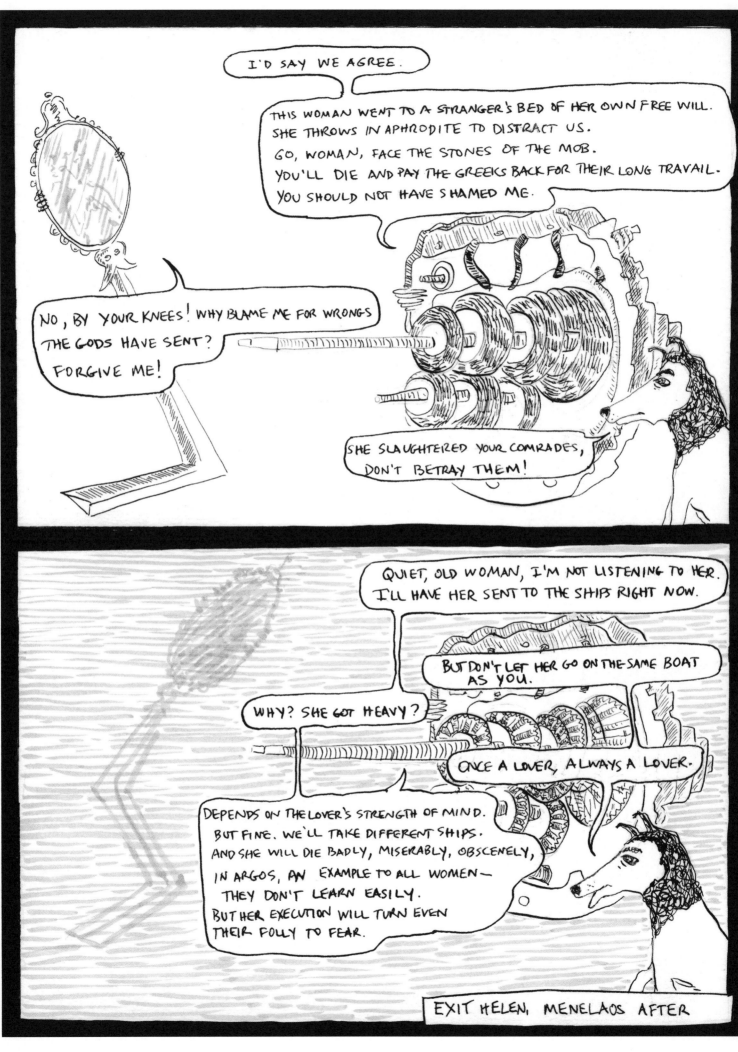

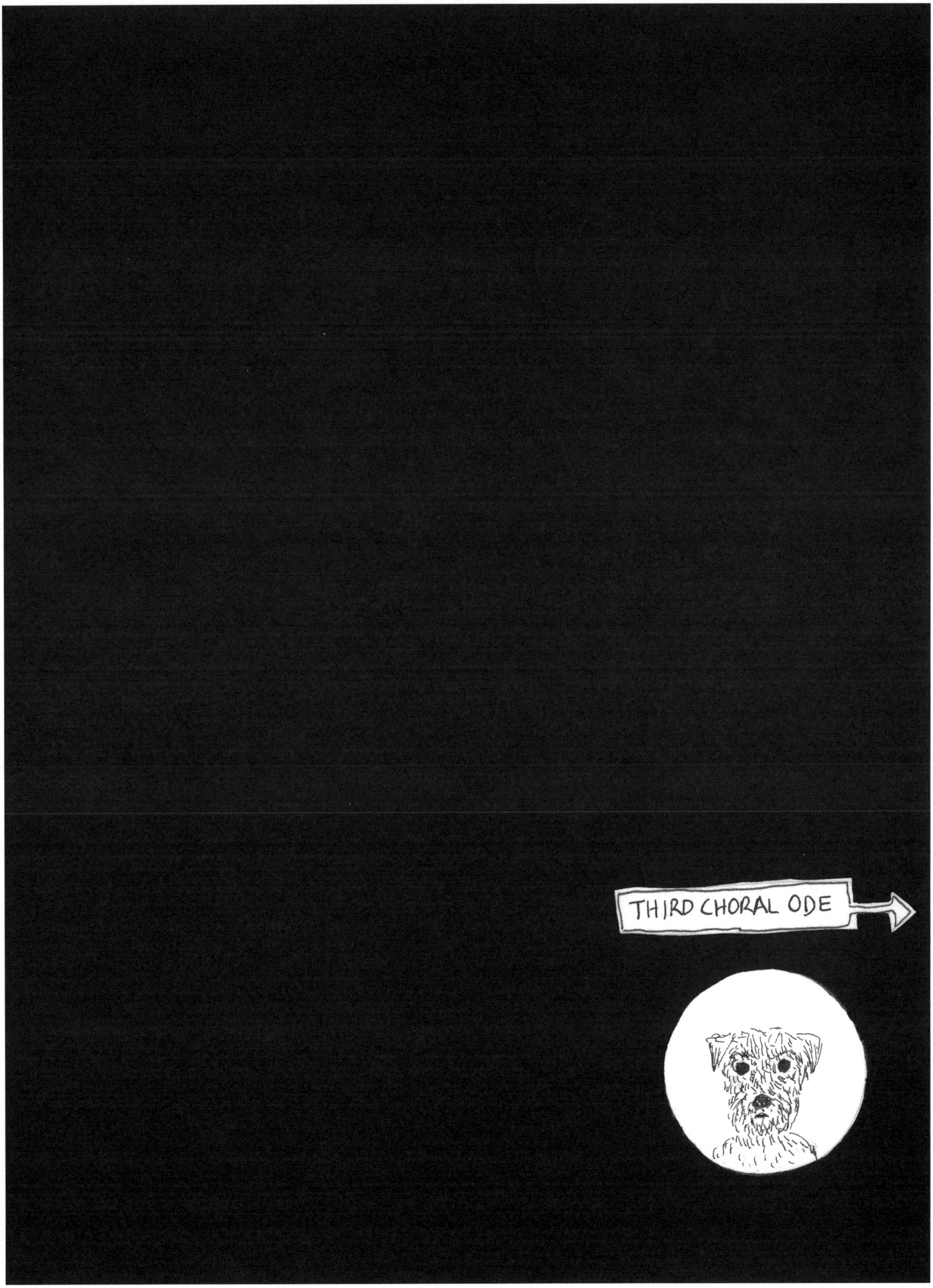
THIRD CHORAL ODE

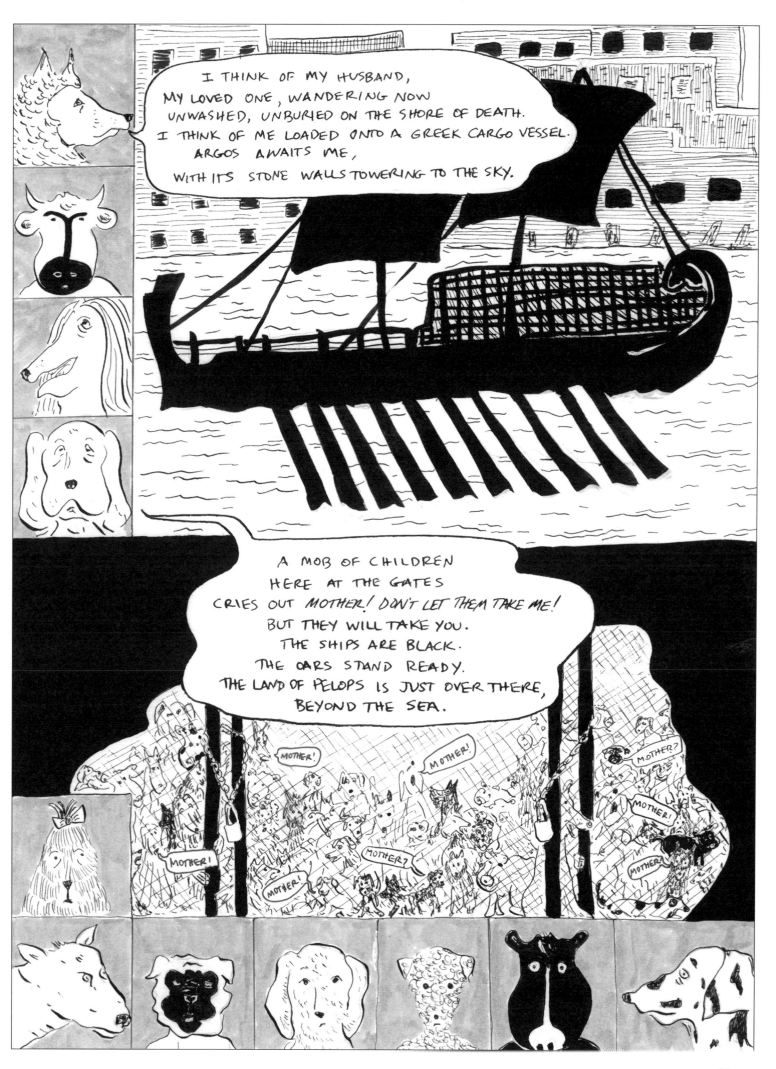

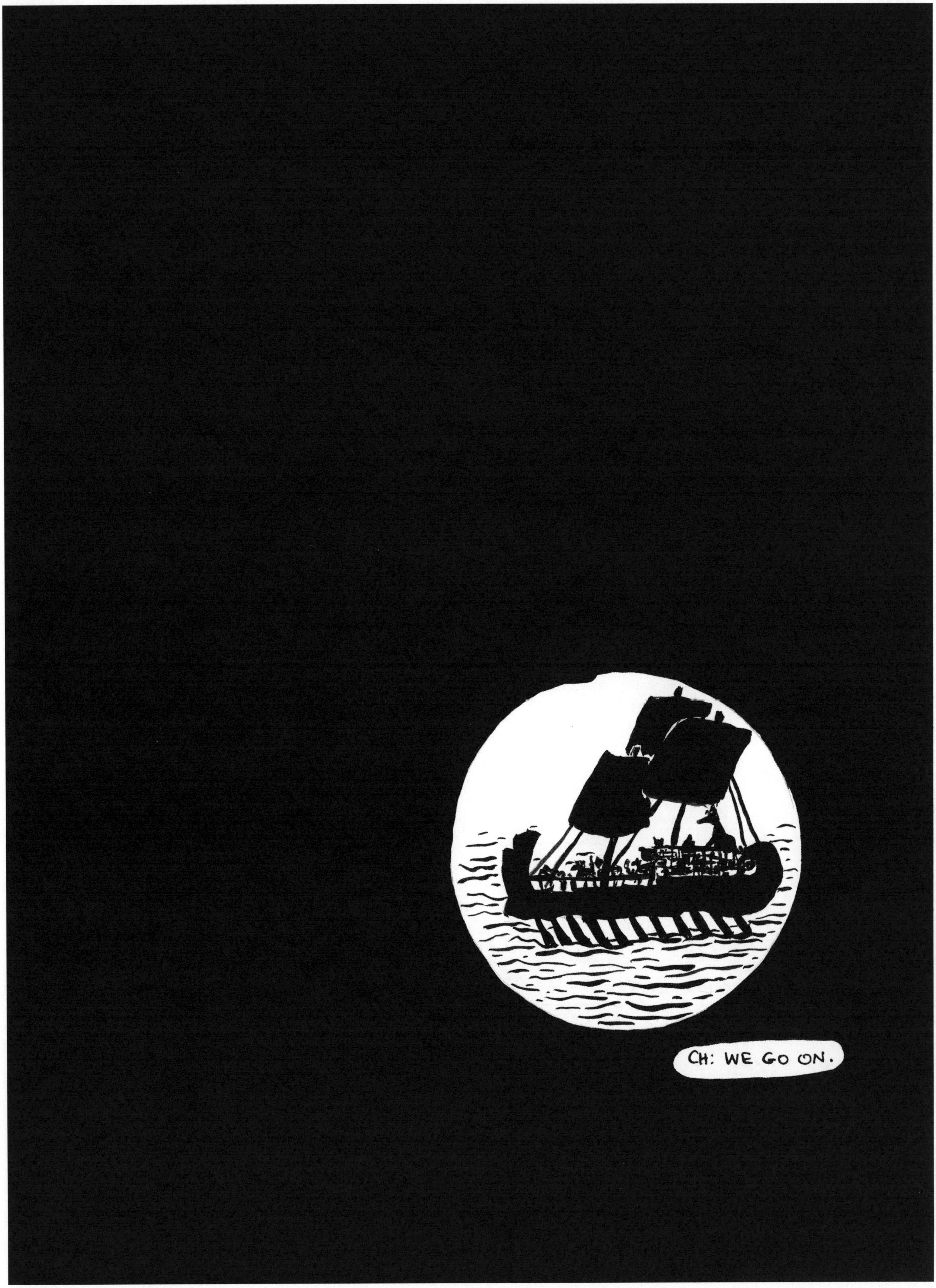
CH: WE GO ON.

ISBN: 978 1 78037 590 8

First published 2021 in the UK by
Bloodaxe Books Ltd
Eastburn
South Park
Hexham
Northumberland NE46 1BS

and by New Directions Publishing Corporation in the USA.

www.bloodaxebooks.com

For further information about Bloodaxe titles
please visit our website and join our mailing list
or write to the above address for a catalogue.

Supported using public funding by
**ARTS COUNCIL
ENGLAND**

Printed in Great Britain by Bell & Bain Limited, Glasgow, Scotland,
on acid-free paper sourced from mills with FSC chain of custody certification.

MIX
Paper from
responsible sources
FSC® C007785